PEOPLE
IN THE NEWS

J.K. Rowling

by Bradley Steffens

LUCENT BOOKS
SAN DIEGO, CALIFORNIA

THOMSON
————✳————™
GALE

Detroit • New York • San Diego • San Francisco
Boston • New Haven, Conn. • Waterville, Maine
London • Munich

Titles in the People in the News series include:

Drew Barrymore	Stephen King
Garth Brooks	George Lucas
George W. Bush	Rosie O'Donnell
Jim Carrey	Brad Pitt
Michael Crichton	Colin Powell
Matt Damon	Princess Diana
Celine Dion	Prince William
Michael J. Fox	Christopher Reeve
Bill Gates	The Rolling Stones
Mel Gibson	Steven Spielberg
John Grisham	R.L. Stine
Jesse Jackson	Oprah Winfrey
Michael Jordan	Tiger Woods

For John,
who first shared the magic of Harry Potter with me

Library of Congress Cataloging-in-Publication Data

Steffens, Bradley
  J.K. Rowling / by Bradley Steffens.
    p. cm. — (People in the news)
Includes bibliographical references and index.
Summary: Examines the personal life and professional career of the author of the best-selling Harry Potter novels.
  ISBN 1-56006-776-4 (hardback : alk. paper)
  1. Rowling, J.K.—Juvenile literature. 2. Authors, English—20th century—Biography—Juvenile literature. 3. Potter, Harry (Fictitious character)—Juvenile literature. 4. Children's stories—Authorship—Juvenile literature. [1. Rowling, J.K. 2. Authors, English. 3. Women—Biography. 4. Potter, Harry (Fictitious character)] I. Title. II. People in the news (San Diego, Calif.)
  PR6068.093 Z86 2002
  823' .914—dc21

2001005248

Table of Contents

Foreword

FAME AND CELEBRITY are alluring. People are drawn to those who walk in fame's spotlight, whether they are known for great accomplishments or for notorious deeds. The lives of the famous pique public interest and attract attention, perhaps because their experiences seem in some ways so different from, yet in other ways so similar to, our own.

Newspapers, magazines, and television regularly capitalize on this fascination with celebrity by running profiles of famous people. For example, television programs such as *Entertainment Tonight* devote all of their programming to stories about entertainment and entertainers. Magazines such as *People* fill their pages with stories of the private lives of famous people. Even newspapers, newsmagazines, and television news frequently delve into the lives of well-known personalities. Despite the number of articles and programs, few provide more than a superficial glimpse at their subjects.

Lucent's People in the News series offers young readers a deeper look into the lives of today's newsmakers, the influences that have shaped them, and the impact they have had in their fields of endeavor and on other people's lives. The subjects of the series hail from many disciplines and walks of life. They include authors, musicians, athletes, political leaders, entertainers, entrepreneurs, and others who have made a mark on modern life and who, in many cases, will continue to do so for years to come.

These biographies are more than factual chronicles. Each book emphasizes the contributions, accomplishments, or deeds that have brought fame or notoriety to the individual and shows how that person has influenced modern life. Authors portray their subjects in a realistic, unsentimental light. For example, Bill Gates—the cofounder and chief executive officer of the software giant Microsoft—has been instrumental in making personal computers the most vital tool of the modern age. Few dispute his business savvy, his perseverance, or his technical expertise, yet critics say he is ruthless in his dealings with competitors and driven more by his desire to maintain Microsoft's dominance in the computer industry than by an interest in furthering technology.

In these books, young readers will encounter inspiring stories about real people who achieved success despite enormous obstacles. Oprah Winfrey—the most powerful, most watched, and wealthiest woman on television today—spent the first six years of her life in the care of her grandparents while her unwed mother sought work and a better life elsewhere. Her adolescence was colored by promiscuity, pregnancy at age fourteen, rape, and sexual abuse.

Each author documents and supports his or her work with an array of primary and secondary source quotations taken from diaries, letters, speeches, and interviews. All quotes are footnoted to show readers exactly how and where biographers derive their information and provide guidance for further research. The quotations enliven the text by giving readers eyewitness views of the life and accomplishments of each person covered in the People in the News series.

In addition, each book in the series includes photographs, annotated bibliographies, timelines, and comprehensive indexes. For both the casual reader and the student researcher, the People in the News series offers insight into the lives of today's newsmakers—people who shape the way we live, work, and play in the modern age.

Introduction

"I'm Not Going to Be Famous"

SHORTLY AFTER SIGNING her first publishing contract in 1996, J.K. Rowling met with her literary agent and executives from her publishing company for lunch. During the meeting, Rowling's business associates cautioned the first-time author not to get her hopes up about making a lot of money from her book. "When I got into this, my agent said to me, 'I don't want you going away from this meeting thinking you're going to make a fortune,'" Rowling recalled. "Then I said to him, 'I know I'm not going to make any money out of it. I know I'm not going to be famous.' All I ever wanted was for somebody to publish Harry so I could go to bookshops and see it."[1]

No author has harbored more modest goals or hazarded a more spectacularly inaccurate prediction of his or her success than J.K. Rowling did that afternoon. Her book would appear not just in her local bookshop but in countless retail outlets around the world, becoming one of the best-selling books of all time. And it would not be her lone success. Three more books would follow in four years, each outselling the one that came before. Along the way, J.K. Rowling would become a household name. Not only would she meet the queen of England, the prince of Wales, and a host of other dignitaries and celebrities, but she would become a celebrity herself. Her image would appear in countless newspapers, books, and magazines. She would be interviewed on television and radio and in Internet chats. On a crisp fall day in October 2000, fifteen thousand fans would

J.K. Rowling has a warm conversation with winners of a Scholastic Press essay contest. Entrants described how the Harry Potter books had changed their lives.

show up at a baseball stadium to listen as she read from one of her books.

By early 2002, Rowling's four books had been translated into forty-eight different languages and sold a staggering 135 million copies worldwide. *Harry Potter and the Sorcerer's Stone,* the first motion picture made from one of her books, had grossed more than $930 million, making it the second highest grossing film of all time.

As amazing as such statistics are, they merely hint at Rowling's most remarkable achievement: her ability to reach, challenge, and entertain one individual reader after another. As *Time* magazine's Paul Gray observed, "Any assessment of her extraordinary impact should focus principally on the private transaction, as old as storytelling, between the speaker and the listener, or a more recent innovation, the writer and the reader. Here, in the hush of imagination, is where Rowling works her magic."[2]

Some of Rowling's readers have written back to her, revealing how their lives have been touched by her words. In an essay submitted to Scholastic Press's "How the Harry Potter Books Changed My Life" contest, nine-year-old Tyler Walton, who suffers from leukemia, wrote, "I sometimes think of Harry Potter and me as being kind of alike. He was forced into situations he couldn't control and had to face an enemy that he didn't know if he could beat." Walton drew strength from his fictional hero, adding, "Harry Potter helped me get through some really hard and scary times."[3]

Fifteen-year-old Ashley Marie Rhodes-Courter, who had been shuffled from one foster home to another, also felt a kinship with the orphaned wizard. "Harry has a lightning scar on his forehead to remind him of his past," she wrote in her Scholastic entry. "There's one on my back to remind me of mine."[4]

In her entry to the "Letters About Literature" contest sponsored by the Library of Congress Center for the Book, twelve-year-old Alaina Alderson of Chugiak, Alaska, told how another of Rowling's books drew her out of a self-imposed isolation:

> I didn't like reading. . . . I was an F student, hated school and was bored all the time. . . . Kids called me names because they thought I was stupid. In school, I just sat pretending I was someplace else. I didn't do any work. . . . I didn't care about anything anymore, including myself. Life was just a big hole. I failed fourth grade. . . .
>
> One day, my grandma dropped a book on my bed and said knowingly, "Read a few pages."
>
> I read more than a few pages. I read more like four chapters. . . . I found a character known as Hermione Granger. When I thought about it, I knew I wanted to be like her. . . .
>
> My life had suddenly changed. From F's and D's to A's and B's, I really felt successful. I enjoyed learning new things. I had nice friends. . . . I loved school, but most of all, I loved to read![5]

Essays and letters like these flood into the offices of Rowling, her publishers, and contest sponsors every day. Such stories are the most dramatic examples of something that happens to millions of Rowling's readers, young and old alike. They begin to sense that the world is filled with unseen possibilities and startling truths—a precious and mysterious place accessible through the most amazing portal of all, the pure and certain power of one's own mind.

Chapter 1

Young Storyteller

ON A NINE-HOUR train trip from King's Cross station in London, England, to a naval base in Arbroath, Scotland, two eighteen-year-old members of the Royal Navy, Anne Volant and Peter Rowling, had the kind of chance encounter often described as magical: They met, spoke, and took an instant liking to each other. Soon their liking grew into love, and love led to marriage. Twenty-five years later, a product of that happy union, a grown daughter named Joanne, would leave King's Cross station on a life-changing journey of her own. Her magical encounter would not be with a flesh-and-blood human being, however, but with a dreamlike figure who would stroll into her "head fully formed"[6]—an imaginary boy whose story she would feel compelled to write. Embarking on this endeavor would not be a new experience for Rowling. She had been telling stories almost from the time she had learned to talk.

Sundridge Park

A few months after they met in 1964, Volant and Rowling each left the Royal Navy. On March 14, 1965, they married. Peter Rowling found work as an apprentice production engineer at the Bristol Siddeley aircraft engine factory in Bristol. Anne Rowling did not look for work outside the home. Instead, she prepared for the birth of her first child.

Rather than live in the city, the Rowlings settled in the small town of Yate, ten miles northeast of Bristol. Inhabited by the Romans as early as the second century B.C., Yate derives its name from the Saxon word *gete,* meaning gate or gateway, for the ancient town stood at the entrance to a large forest. By the time the Rowlings moved to Yate, however, most of the forest was gone, cleared to make way for agriculture and the mining of various materials—limestone to the east of town, coal to the west, and the mineral celestine, or spar, near the center.

The Rowlings moved into a modest home at 109 Sundridge Park, a gently curving street not far from the River Frome, which winds through the center of town. The area is built up now, but in the 1960s it was mostly open land. "This was fields all around when we first came here,"[7] remembered Alan Hall, a former

Chipping Sodbury or Yate?

In her online autobiography *The Not Especially Fascinating Life So Far of JK Rowling*, J.K. Rowling stated, "I was born in Chipping Sodbury General Hospital, which I think is appropriate for someone who collects funny names." Because this information came directly from Rowling, dozens of reporters repeated it in their news articles, hundreds of Web masters posted it on their websites, and thousands of students included it in their book reports and theme papers. Oddly enough, it was not true.

On July 18, 2000, a Bristol newspaper published a copy of Rowling's birth certificate. It showed that Rowling was born at Cottage Hospital in Yate. Biographer Sean Smith reproduced the document in his book *J.K. Rowling: A Biography*. He wrote, "J.K. Rowling has often said that she hails from Chipping Sodbury. . . . The only problem was . . . Rowling was not actually born in Chipping Sodbury and never lived there."

In her review of Smith's book for the *Sunday Herald,* Melanie McDonagh called his "revelation" about Rowling's birthplace "a bit thin." In addition, an article from *Sunday on Scotland* appearing on The Wizard World website reported that "a spokeswoman for Rowling said the author was 'well aware' of [Smith's] book but had 'absolutely no intention of reading it.' She said Rowling was 'furious' it had been written after she had co-operated with a previous biography."

Since a birth certificate is a public record, Rowling would seem to have little reason to complain about its publication. And it is not surprising that the public would wonder why she published the false account of her birthplace in the first place. Did she make an honest mistake? Was she influenced by what Smith calls the "snob appeal" that makes "a Chipping Sodbury postal address . . . worth much gold"? Did she prefer Chipping Sodbury to Yate because it appealed to her love of odd names?

Rowling has refused to comment on the matter.

neighbor of the Rowlings. Anne and Peter Rowling enjoyed the rustic setting and often took sightseeing tours around the neighborhood. A short walk from the Rowlings' home stands Stanshawes Court, a three-story Victorian manor built in 1874. The massive stone building, now a hotel, overlooks the entrance to Kingsgate Park, a wooded area containing two small lakes that was once part of the manor's grounds. Small enough to freeze over in the winter, the lakes provide a nesting area for many species of birds in the summer.

Also within walking distance of the Rowlings' home was Cottage Hospital, located at 240 Station Road. It was here that Anne Rowling gave birth to her first child, a girl, on July 31, 1965. The Rowlings named their baby Joanne.

Less than two years later, on June 28, 1967, Anne gave birth to a second child, this time at home. Joanne Rowling later recalled the event:

> My earliest memory is of my sister being born—she's just under two years younger than me. My dad gave me Play-Doh the day she arrived, to keep me occupied while he ran in and out of the bedroom. I have no memory of seeing the new baby, but I do remember eating the Play-Doh.[8]

Like her older sister, the second Rowling daughter was given a name that contained her mother's name—Dianne. From the time they were born, Joanne and Dianne Rowling were almost always called by their nicknames, Jo and Di.

"I Just Remember the Book"

The Rowling girls were inseparable. They played together, watched cartoons together, and listened to stories their parents read to them. Anne and Peter Rowling were avid readers who exposed their children to books at an early age. "My most vivid memory of childhood is my father sitting and reading *Wind in the Willows* to me," Rowling later said. "I had measles at the time, very badly, but I don't remember that; I just remember the book."[9]

Like many elder siblings, Rowling took the lead in choosing what games she and Di would play. Recalling that she was

As a youngster, Rowling invented stories about animals. Her first written story told the tale of a rabbit, a creature beloved by Rowling and her sister.

somewhat bossy as a child, Rowling later confessed that she forced her sister to listen to stories that she made up: "She was the person who suffered my first efforts at story-telling (I was much bigger than her and could hold her down)."[10]

Many of Rowling's childhood stories involved animals, especially rabbits, which both children loved. One story featured a main character named Di who fell down a hole and was fed fresh strawberries by a rabbit family. Di wanted to hear her sister's stories over and over but complained whenever she changed them. To solve the problem, Rowling began to write her stories down. "The first story I ever wrote down (when I was five or six) was about a rabbit called Rabbit," Rowling recalled. "He got the measles and was visited by his friends, including a giant bee called Miss Bee." Rowling enjoyed writing so much that she made a secret decision to pursue it as a career. "Ever since Rabbit and Miss Bee," she later said, "I have wanted to be a writer, though I rarely told anyone so."[11]

The Potters

About the time Rowling began writing the Rabbit stories, Peter and Anne Rowling bought their first home, a three-bedroom house at 35 Nicholls Lane in Winterbourne, four miles from Yate. Several families lived on Nicholls Lane, including one with a name that would linger in Rowling's imagination for years—the Potters.

Graham and Ruby Potter had two children: Ian and Vicki. Ian Potter was no wizard, but he did have a great sense of humor and a flair for mischief. He once placed a slug on a plate and tried to convince Rowling it was a delectable treat. Another time he tricked the Rowling girls into leaving their footprints in wet cement. The children often played outdoors, but according to Ian their favorite activity was dressing up. "Nine times out of ten," he later told *Book* magazine, "it would be Joanne who had the idea, and she'd always say, 'Can't we be witches and wizards?'"[12]

Although life in Winterbourne was pleasant, Rowling's father was always looking for better opportunities for his family. At one point, he considered moving the family to Canada. "When I was about eight years old," Rowling later told a Canadian radio interviewer, "my father was offered the opportunity to come and work here for a year." The entire family was excited by the prospect of moving to the faraway land. "For a moment we thought we really were coming to live in Canada, and we were very excited," Rowling recalled. The offer fell through, however, leaving the Rowlings "very disappointed."[13]

Church Cottage

Within a year, the family did move—not across the ocean but across the River Severn to the village of Tutshill, located in the Forest of Dean. It was here that Peter and Anne Rowling discovered an affordable home with a view of the River Wye. Peter Rowling had always wanted to fix up an older home, and he got his wish when he and Anne found Church Cottage for sale. Built in 1848, the stone structure had served as Tutshill's school until

When the Rowling family moved to Church Cottage, their home had a
view of the River Wye, pictured here flowing through the Forest of Dean.

a larger school was built nearby in 1893. The Rowlings sold their
house in Winterbourne, purchased Church Cottage, and began
to convert it into their dream home.

   In the fall of 1974, Joanne Rowling donned the blue-on-blue
uniform of the Tutshill Church of England Primary School and
took the short walk to her new school. Tutshill Primary was a
small, old-fashioned school where the antique rolltop desks still
had inkwells. It was here that the nine-year-old Rowling met
another person who would leave an impression on her, Mrs.
Sylvia Morgan.

   On Rowling's first day at the new school, Morgan gave her
a test to determine her academic rank. The test included frac-
tions, which Rowling had not yet learned. Rowling did not get a
single problem correct. Afterward, Morgan told Rowling to sit
at a desk on the right side of the class. Rowling did not know it
at the time, but Morgan assigned seats based on how intelligent

she thought her students were. "The brightest sat on her left, and everyone she thought was dim sat on the right," Rowling recalled. "I was as far right as you could get without sitting in the playground."[14]

Rowling worked hard to prove that she was smarter than her teacher thought she was. Her efforts paid off. "By the end of the year, I had been promoted to second left," Rowling remembered, "but at a cost. Mrs. Morgan made me swap seats with my best friend, so that in one short walk across the room I became clever but unpopular."[15]

"Life's Ambition"

Away from school, Rowling spent much of her free time walking through the fields and along the River Wye with her sister. She also read for pleasure, delving into books intended for children as well as for adults. By the time she was nine, she was reading Ian Fleming's novels about the spy James Bond. She also began to read novels by the nineteenth-century English novelist Jane Austen, a keen observer of human behavior who often wrote about pairs of sisters coming of age. "My favorite writer is Jane Austen, and I've read all her books so many times I've lost count,"[16] Rowling later disclosed in an interview. Rowling also enjoyed works by Elizabeth Goudge, C.S. Lewis, Paul Gallico, and Edith Nesbit:

> My favorite book when I was about 8 was [Goudge's] *The Little White Horse,* and the heroine, Maria, because she was a very interesting heroine—she wasn't beautiful, she was nosy, she had a temper. She was human, in a word, when a lot of girl characters tend not to be. I really like Eustace in *The Voyage of the Dawn Treader* by C.S. Lewis. He is a very unlikable character who turns good. He is one of C.S. Lewis's funniest characters, and I like him a lot. . . . A book I loved when I was younger was Paul Gallico's *Manxmouse,* which is a funny, magical, very imaginative book. I really loved it. . . . I also liked anything by E. Nesbit. Anything by her! Her life and everything just strikes a chord with me.[17]

Rowling especially enjoyed C.S. Lewis's Narnia books. "Even now, if I was in a room with one of the Narnia books I would pick it up like a shot and re-read it,"[18] she later told Helena de Bertodano of the *Daily Telegraph*.

Rowling began to emulate the writers she loved, fashioning stories and creating characters with unusual names. She rarely shared her work with anyone other than Di, who was a constant source of encouragement. "My life's ambition has been to write full time," she later told *School Library Journal*. "This is all I have wanted from the age of six. I cannot overstate how much I wanted that. But I didn't talk about it at all. I just never really spoke about it, because I was embarrassed. And because my parents were the kind of parents who would have thought, 'Ah yes, that's very nice, dear. But where is the pension plan?'"[19]

Wyedean Comprehensive School

After graduating from Tutshill Primary School in 1976, Rowling started sixth grade at Wyedean Comprehensive School. Surrounded by more mature students, the eleven-year-old Rowling found herself feeling insecure. On top of everything else, Rowling faced the changes of puberty, which made her feel self-conscious. She later described herself during this time as "a pudding-faced child, with glasses, and rather studious, a shy, snotty, swotty little kid, and very insecure."[20]

Despite her shortcomings, Rowling made friends with other bookish students, whom she often entertained by telling stories. "I used to tell my equally quiet and studious friends long serial stories at lunch-times," she remembered. "They usually involved us all doing heroic and daring deeds we certainly wouldn't have done in real life." Rowling wrote some stories down, but mostly kept them to herself. "I wrote a lot in my teens, but I never showed any of it to my friends," Rowling recalled, "except for funny stories that again featured us all in thinly disguised characters."[21]

Several of Rowling's teachers noticed her writing ability and did their best to encourage the teenager to develop her creative talents. Her greatest inspiration did not come from one of her teachers, however; it came from her great-aunt. When Rowling was fourteen, her great-aunt Ivy told her about

As a young girl, Rowling admired Jessica Mitford (pictured) for her social activism and strength of character.

Jessica Mitford, a social activist who ran away from home as a teenager. "You know what she did, Jo," Rowling recalled her aunt saying, "she bought a camera on her father's account and then went traveling."[22]

Rowling admired Mitford's adventurous spirit. Later she came across Mitford's autobiography, *Hons and Rebels,* and was further impressed by the activist's independence, courage, and strength. "She lost two of her four kids in tragic circumstances—and yet she had no self-pity and a fabulous sense of humor right to the bitter end,"[23] Rowling later observed. Inspired by Mitford, Rowling decided that she, too, would try to right the world's wrongs and work for social change.

Rowling shared her aspirations with only a few close friends. One of these was Sean P.F. Harris, a thoughtful young man who would remain one of Rowling's best friends throughout her life. Rowling did not own a car or know how to drive, but Harris did. Together they explored the discos, concerts, and teenage hangouts in Bristol, Bath, and other cities. Later, Rowling would dedicate her second book to Harris, referring to him as her "getaway driver and foulweather friend."[24]

Who Was Jessica Mitford?

When J.K. Rowling was fourteen, her great-aunt Ivy inspired her with the story of Jessica Mitford. One of six sisters, Mitford was born into an aristocratic family in Gloucestershire, England, in 1917. Her sister Unity was a fascist who moved to Germany and became a personal friend of Nazi leader Adolf Hitler. Another sister, Diana, married the leader of England's fascist political party. Jessica was appalled by her sisters' beliefs and chose to associate herself with socialism.

While a teenager, Mitford was inspired by the antifascist writings of Esmond Romilly, a nephew of Winston Churchill. Reading that Romilly was fighting against the fascists in the Spanish Civil War, Mitford gathered up the money she had saved for running away and headed off to Spain. Her father, a member of the House of Lords, sent members of the British navy to retrieve her, but she refused to return to England.

Mitford arrived in Spain and eventually met Romilly. The two ended up falling in love and marrying. The couple came to the United States in 1939. When World War II broke out, Romilly joined the Canadian Air Force. Less than a year after the birth of their daughter, his plane went down over the North Sea in 1941.

A twenty-four-year-old widow with an infant daughter, Mitford started her new life. She married a labor lawyer named Bob Treuhaft in 1943 and the couple moved to California, where they joined the Communist Party.

In the 1950s, Mitford began a career as a writer. In 1960, she published her autobiography, *Hons and Rebels*. She followed this book with a critical look at the funeral industry titled *The American Way of Death*. This book catapulted Mitford to fame as a muckraker. She continued to write and teach until her death in 1996. Her books include *Kind and Usual Punishment: The Prison Business* (1973), *A Fine Old Conflict* (1979), and *Poison Penmanship: The Gentle Art of Muckraking* (1979).

As Rowling identified goals for her life and made new friends, she gained confidence and became more popular. She continued to get good grades as well. Respected by classmates and teachers alike, Rowling was voted "head girl" of her graduating class.

Exeter

In June 1983, seventeen-year-old Joanne Rowling graduated from Wyedean Comprehensive with honors. She did not take a year off between high school and college, which is a common practice in Britain. Instead, she enrolled that fall in Exeter University and majored in foreign languages, a decision she later regretted. "I went to Exeter University straight after school, where I studied French," she recalled. "This was a big mistake. I had listened too hard to my parents, who thought languages would lead to a great career as a bilingual secretary."[25]

Rowling may have had regrets about her course of study, but while at Exeter she learned valuable lessons about herself and the world around her. For the first time in her life, she began to make major decisions on her own. When the opportunity to study in France arose, Rowling took it. Her first trip abroad added to her growing confidence. Not only did she study while in Paris, but she gained valuable experience as a student teacher. While at Exeter, Rowling also fell in love, beginning a relationship that would last for several years.

Although her studies did not leave Rowling a great deal of free time, she continued to write. She tried her hand at poetry,

The chapel and library of Exeter University. While attending school here, Rowling began to assert her independence.

short stories, and drama. She even began work on a novel, which she nearly completed before abandoning it. This false start was far from a failure, however. Rowling was learning important lessons about plot, characterization, and dialogue. Rowling kept her writing mainly to herself, showing her work only to her boyfriend, Di, and a few others. Those closest to her encouraged her to share her writing with the world, but Rowling refused to submit her work for publication.

Inspiration

Rowling graduated with honors from Exeter in 1987. Shortly after, she, along with other Exeter graduates, moved to London to pursue a career, renting a flat in Clapham in southwest London. Inspired by the example of Jessica Mitford, Rowling sought work with the human rights organization Amnesty International. She was hired as a research assistant studying human rights abuses in French-speaking Africa. In her free time, Rowling began to work on a second novel. She often spent her lunch hours at cafés, working on her manuscript.

At first, Rowling felt satisfied with her job at Amnesty International. She was supporting herself and having a positive impact on the world. Eventually, however, Rowling grew tired of the job. She did not have the temperament to sit in an office and do research. She longed to work on the front lines of social change, but this was not possible for a newcomer such as herself. Disenchanted, Rowling resigned from her job at Amnesty International after just two years.

Not sure what to do, Rowling began to look for work as a bilingual secretary—the career her parents had suggested. She landed several jobs, but ended up leaving each one. By her own admission, she was not a good secretary. "I had some office jobs, and anyone who worked with me will tell you that I was the most disorganized person that ever walked this earth," Rowling later told an interviewer. "I wasn't good. I'm *not* proud of that. I don't think it's charming and eccentric. I really should have been better at it, but I really am just all over the place when it comes to organizing myself."[26] She also abandoned the novel she had been working on.

Amnesty International

Rowling spent two years working for Amnesty International, hoping to contribute to the world the way that her heroine, Jessica Mitford, did. Amnesty International (AI) campaigns for human rights. According to the organization's website, its focus is to do the following:

- free all prisoners of conscience. According to AI's Statute, these are people detained for their political, religious or other conscientiously held beliefs or because of their ethnic origin, sex, colour, language, national or social origin, economic status, birth or other status—who have not used or advocated violence;

- ensure fair and prompt trials for all political prisoners;

- abolish the death penalty, torture and other ill-treatment of prisoners;

- end political killings and "disappearances";

- end abuses by armed political groups such as detention of prisoners of conscience, hostage-taking, torture and unlawful killings;

- end grave abuses of human rights by non-state actors, such as those committed against women in the family or the community, where it can be shown that the state has failed to act with due diligence.

Rowling had hoped that her work for Amnesty International, researching complaints of violations, would prove to be as exciting and adventurous as she understood Jessica Mitford's work to be. Rowling was disappointed to discover that the work was largely clerical, and rather tedious. After two years with the organization, she resigned.

With her career stalled in London, Rowling began to consider moving to Manchester, England's second largest city, where her college boyfriend had settled. She began to spend her weekends in Manchester, visiting her boyfriend and looking for an apartment. After one of these visits in June 1990, Rowling gazed out the window of the train she was taking back to King's Cross station in London and began to daydream. Suddenly, in her mind's eye she saw a boy with dark hair, green eyes, glasses, and a mark on his forehead in the shape of a lightning bolt. Rowling did not yet know the young man's name, but she had just met Harry Potter.

Chapter 2

The Growth of an Idea

T HE TRAIN ROWLING was taking from Manchester to London in June 1990 broke down in the middle of the English country-side. During the delay, Rowling began to imagine all kinds of things about the boy she had pictured. He was a wizard. Not a full-fledged wizard, but a wizard in the making, a boy who did not understand his own powers. He would have to go through special training. Wizard training. At a school of witchcraft and wizardry. The trickle of ideas turned into a stream, then a torrent. Rowling searched for a working pen, but found none. When the train resumed its journey, Rowling strained to remember each detail. "Rather than try to write it, I had to think it," she later recalled. "And I think that was a very good thing. I was besieged by a mass of detail, and if it didn't survive that journey, it probably wasn't worth remembering."[27]

"This Massive Rush"

Back at her flat, Rowling wrote down everything she could remember about the young wizard and his adventures. She worked in a frenzy of inspiration, she later explained:

> I had this physical reaction to it, this huge rush of adrenaline, which is always a sign that you've had a good idea, when you've a physical response, this massive rush, and I'd never felt that before. I'd had ideas I liked, but never quite so powerful. And Harry came first, in this huge rush. Doesn't know he's a wizard, how can he not know? And, very bizarrely, he had a mark on his forehead, but I didn't know why at that point. It was like research. It didn't feel as if I were entirely inventing it.[28]

Remembering the difficulties she encountered with her two unfinished novels, Rowling did not immediately start writing the first chapter of her imagined book. Instead, she made notes, sketched characters, and plotted the story. She reviewed the lists of names she had collected through the years, trying to match them up with the characters she created. She wanted to have the project thought through completely before she started writing. Little did she know that this process would take not weeks or months but years.

Rowling immediately realized that all of her imaginings would not fit in a single book. Even before she got off the train, Rowling had envisioned a seven-book series, one book for each year that her wizard-in-training would spend in school. The practical aspects of selling a seven-book series were the furthest thing from Rowling's mind. "When you dream, you can do what you like. And I always thought seven was a good number."[29]

Not long after conceiving her story, Rowling took a clerical job with the Manchester Chamber of Commerce. She split her free time between the two men in her life—her boyfriend and the boy wizard she decided to name Harry Potter. Instead of spending her lunch hours with her coworkers, Rowling stole

Rowling's rich imagination provided her with an astonishing amount of detail about the fledgling wizard she had envisioned.

away to nearby cafés to work on her growing collection of notes and sketches.

"I'm Writing Fantasy!"

At first, Rowling did not give much thought to the genre of story she was imagining. "It didn't occur to me for quite a while that I was writing fantasy," she later said. For Rowling, wizardry simply offered a way to empower her young hero and allow him to escape from his stifling existence as the unwanted ward of his aunt and uncle. "There's a small part of you that wishes you could alter external things to be the way they ought to be," she observed. "That's why there will always, always, always be books about magic, discovering secret powers, stuff that you're not allowed to do."[30]

To support this story line, Rowling created a magical world that exists side by side with—and slightly overlaps—the world of ordinary human beings, which she decided to call Muggles. Only after she had populated this alternate world with enchanted characters and fantastic beasts did Rowling realize what kind of story she was writing. "I was about two thirds of the way through, and I suddenly thought, 'This has got unicorns in it. I'm writing fantasy!'"[31]

Rowling knew that, for such a story to work, she would need to give her fictional world enough detail to make readers feel that they had stepped into a real place. Rowling approached this task with the same dedication that she had applied to her schoolwork years before. Throughout the summer of 1990, she spent hours mapping out the school where Harry Potter would learn his craft. "Hogwarts School of Witchcraft and Wizardry was the first thing I concentrated on," Rowling recalled. "I was thinking of a place of great order, but immense danger, with children who had skill with which to overwhelm their teachers. Logically it had to be set in a secluded place, and pretty soon I settled on Scotland in my mind. I think it was a subconscious tribute to where my parents had married."[32]

Hogwarts emerged as a Byzantine structure, several stories high, replete with enchanted staircases and secret passageways. When asked if she had sketched out a floor plan of Hogwarts to

Good Versus Evil

From the outset, J.K. Rowling saw the story of Harry Potter as a conflict between good and evil. As she developed her story, Rowling faced choices about how deeply and realistically to portray evil, especially if the story would be read by children. She later told Roxanne Feldman of *School Library Journal* how she decided to proceed:

> If you are writing about Good and Evil, there comes a point where you have to get serious. This is something I really have had to think about. Early on, I had to consider how to depict an evil being, such as Lord Voldemort [in books one and two]. I could go one of two ways: I could either make him a pantomime villian . . . [meaning that there is] a lot of sound and thunder and nobody really gets hurt. Or [I could] attempt to do something a little bit more serious—which means you're going to have to show death. And worse than that, you'll have to show the death of characters whom the readers care about. I chose the second route.

In an interview with Nigel Ballard of BBC Radio Gloucestershire, Rowling explained that she felt a moral obligation to depict evil in an honest, forthright way:

> I'm dealing with evil. I'm trying to examine what happens to this community when a maniac tries to take over, with all its ramifications, as in who will be attracted to that side, what happens to the people who are fighting that, and how they themselves become corrupted, and the reality of how evil it is to take a human life and to torture and to attempt control. And if you are going to write about those kinds of things, I think you have a moral obligation to show what that involves and *not* to prettify it or to minimize it.

Once the Harry Potter books were published, many people asked Rowling if her depiction of evil was too menacing for her audience. "Have you ever thought 'Maybe I should tone it down'?" Jeff Jenson of *Entertainment Weekly* asked Rowling. She replied:

> No. I know that sounds kind of brutal but no, I haven't. The bottom line is, I have to write the story I want to write. I never wrote them with a focus group of 8 year olds in mind. I have to continue telling the story the way I want to tell it. I don't at all relish the idea of children in tears, and I absolutely don't deny it's frightening. But it's supposed to be frightening! And if you don't show how scary that is, you cannot show how incredibly brave Harry is.

aid in her writing, Rowling replied, "I haven't drawn it, because it would be difficult for the most skilled architect to draw, owing to the fact that the staircases and the rooms keep moving. However, I have a very vivid image of what it looks like."[33]

Rowling chose the name for the school by turning to the lists of unusual names that she had compiled through the years. Ever since childhood, Rowling had jotted down quaint, peculiar, or odd-sounding names she had seen on street signs, maps, war memorials, gravestones, and other places. One important name came to her in a botanical garden. "I thought I made up Hogwarts," Rowling explained, "but recently a friend said, 'Remember we saw lilies in Kew gardens.' Apparently there are lilies there called Hogwarts. I'd forgotten!"[34]

A Poet's Sensitivity

Although Rowling has claimed to have "a slight blind spot about poetry,"[35] she composed the names of her characters and places in her novels with a poet's sensitivity to sound and meaning. She later told an interviewer how she came up with the name of a prominent wizard who is the author of many books:

> Gilderoy Lockhart is a good example. I knew his name had to have an impressive ring to it. I was looking through the *Dictionary of Phrase and Fable*—a great source for names—and came across Gilderoy, a handsome Scottish highwayman. Exactly what I wanted. And then I found Lockhart on a war memorial to the First World War. The two together said everything I wanted about the character.[36]

Rowling sometimes used the root meanings of words to enrich her characters' names. For example, Dumbledore, the name of the headmaster at Hogwarts, is Old English for "bumblebee." She felt the word "seemed to suit the headmaster, because one of his passions is music and I imagined him walking around humming to himself."[37]

Rowling also drew on her knowledge of foreign languages to create distinctive names. For example, she conjured up the name of Lord Voldemort, the evil wizard who killed Harry Potter's parents, by combining two French words, *volonté,* meaning will, and *mort,* meaning death, in what one critic has called "a kind of mock medieval French."[38]

Rowling's knowledge of Latin and Greek also seeped into her work. Critic Maurine Dowd observed,

> Rowling, who studied classics at the University of Exeter, chose names with a Latin ring: Lord Voldemort, Draco and Narcissa Malfoy, Albus Dumbledore, Nimbus 2000, Sibyll Trelawney. She came up with a Latin motto for the Hogwarts School: Draco Dormiens Nunquam Titillandus (Never Tickle a Sleeping Dragon). And she alludes to Cerberus and Orpheus with Fluffy, the three-headed, music-loving dog that guards the sorcerer's stone, and to Proteus with her shape-shifting animagus.[39]

Rowling borrowed the name of one of her most important characters, Hermione Granger, from the works of the English

A memorial bust of William Shakespeare. Rowling borrowed the name for one of her characters, Hermione, from Shakespeare's play The Winter's Tale.

poet and playwright William Shakespeare. "The first play I saw was at Stratford upon Avon," Rowling recalled. "We saw Shakespeare's *King Lear*. I was absolutely electrified by it. We also saw *The Winter's Tale* and that was where I found the name Hermione—although of course it didn't come in handy until years later."[40]

"Complete Histories"

Rowling had to do more than find names for her characters. She also had to develop their personalities. To achieve this, she composed detailed backgrounds for everyone, regardless of whether or not she would later use the material in the book. "I almost always have complete histories for my characters," she later told an interviewer. "Sirius Black is a good example. I have a whole childhood worked out for him. The readers don't need to know that but I do. I need to know more than them because I'm the one moving the characters across the page."[41]

Many authors model their characters on people they know or have known, and Rowling is no exception. To create Harry Potter's close friend Ron Weasley, Rowling borrowed traits from her Wyedean Comprehensive School chum Sean Harris. "Ron

Turquoise Ford Anglia

J.K. Rowling dedicated her second book, *Harry Potter and the Chamber of Secrets*, to her "getaway driver and foulweather friend" Sean Harris. She also admitted in an online interview with *Scholastic.com* that her character "Ron Weasley is a little bit like my oldest friend, a man I was at school with, whose name is Sean."

Not only did Harris make it into Rowling's books, but so did his car. As quoted in Lindsey Fraser's *Conversations with J.K. Rowling*, Rowling, who does not drive, recalled that Sean "had a turquoise Ford Anglia which spelled freedom for me. . . . So you can imagine that I couldn't use just any old car rescuing Harry and Ron Weasley to take them to Hogwarts—it had to be a turquoise Ford Anglia."

A painting of a turquoise Ford Anglia graced the cover of the Bloomsbury edition of *Harry Potter and the Chamber of Secrets*. When Rowling turned up at King's Cross station in London to promote her fourth book, *Harry Potter and the Goblet of Fire*, she arrived in a turquoise Ford Anglia.

Weasley isn't a living portrait of Sean, but he really is very Sean-ish,"[42] Rowling later told an interviewer. Like Weasley, Harris always proved to be a loyal friend and would later come to Rowling's aid at one of the lowest points of her life.

Rowling reached even further back in her life for a model for Professor Snape, the potion master who picks on Harry Potter in class. Recalling her menacing primary school teacher Mrs. Morgan, Rowling would later tell an interviewer, "There are a number of people who influenced the character of Snape in my books, and that teacher was definitely one of them."[43]

Hermione/Her Self

As Rowling pondered her cast of characters, she decided that Harry Potter's inner circle of friends should include at least one girl his own age. Rowling did not have to look outside herself for inspiration for this character, whom she named Hermione Granger. "Hermione was very easy to create because she is based almost entirely on myself at the age of 11," Rowling later told an interviewer. "Like Hermione, I was obsessed with achieving academically, but this masked a huge insecurity. I think it is very common for plain young girls to feel this way." Hermione is passionate about civil rights, calling for the fair treatment of House Elves, just as Rowling was inspired by Jessica Mitford to become a social activist. Rowling insists that at some point the similarities between her and Hermione end and exaggeration takes over. "She really is a caricature of me. I wasn't as clever as she is, nor do I think I was quite such a know-it-all, though former classmates might disagree."[44]

Who Is Harry Potter?

While Rowling has no trouble identifying the inspiration for Hermione Granger, she is hard-pressed to do the same for the black-haired boy with glasses who had arrived in her imagination during that fateful train ride from Manchester to London in June 1990. Rowling admits that she borrowed her hero's surname from her childhood friends Ian and Vicki Potter. "Harry is one of my favorite boy's names," Rowling said. "But he had several different surnames before I chose Potter. Potter was the

The young wizard with black hair and glasses as depicted in the film
Harry Potter and the Sorcerer's Stone.

name of a brother and sister who I played with when I was very
young. We were part of the same gang and I always liked that
surname."[45] Rowling dismisses the idea that Ian was an inspiration for Harry, however. Although Ian Potter was one of Rowling's first male friends and seemed to have had plenty of
derring-do, his outgoing personality and love of pranks mark
him as more of an inspiration for the older Weasley twins than
for Harry.

Harry Potter has a quiet, serious side reminiscent of Rowling
herself. Both the character and his creator share the same birthday—July 31. In addition, it is Harry, not Hermione, who wears
glasses reminiscent of the "very thick National Health glasses

—free glasses that were like bottle bottoms"[46] that Rowling wore as a child.

As she continued to create her lead character, Rowling decided that Harry Potter's cousin Dudley would punch Harry in the nose and break his glasses. Rowling, too, knew what it was like to be on the receiving end of a bully's abuse. While a student at Wyedean, Rowling was attacked by another girl. To the girl's surprise, Rowling fought back. "I didn't have a choice," Rowling recalled, "she started hitting me and it was hit back or lie down and play dead. For a few days I was quite famous because she hadn't managed to flatten me. The truth was that my locker was right behind me and held me up. I spent weeks afterwards peering nervously around corners in case she was waiting to ambush me."[47]

Although Rowling downplays her role in the schoolyard scuffle, her willingness to stand up for herself is reminiscent of one of Harry's most important traits: courage. "I admire bravery above almost every other characteristic," Rowling once said. "Bravery is a very glamorous virtue, but I'm talking about bravery in all sorts of places. It was brave of Harry to answer back to the Dursleys; they had all the cards, and he was standing up for himself even then. That's why I love him so much. He's a fighter."[48]

Harry Potter is by no means a clone of Rowling, however. He differs from her in many important ways. For one thing, Rowling decided to make her young hero a good athlete, something Rowling admits she was not. A natural at flying a broomstick, Harry would prove to be talented at playing the demanding position of seeker for his hall's Quidditch team. By contrast, Rowling managed to break her arm while playing the noncontact sport of netball at Wyedean. "Sport is such an important part of school life," Rowling has said. "I am terrible at all sports, but I gave my hero a talent I'd love to have."[49]

The biggest difference between Harry Potter and Joanne Rowling is that Harry is an orphan whose parents died when he was a baby but Rowling grew up with both parents to care for her and for her to love. Part of Rowling's reason for making Harry an orphan was practical. "All through literature—and not just children's—the hero has been removed from the family setting,"

At Hogwarts, the wizards-in-training learn to fly broomsticks. Here, in a scene from the movie, the character Neville Longbottom takes flight.

Rowling has observed. "It serves the important function of enabling the hero to act without the fear of destroying his family and disappointing people who love him, or—which is very important—having to expect frailties in his parents."[50]

Rowling also realized that making Harry an orphan would cause readers to view him sympathetically. "Harry is smart and good at sports and a lot of things that other children would like to be, but children feel for him because he's lost his parents,"[51] Rowling later observed.

Knowing that a literary character who comes across as perfect is not believable, Rowling took care to give Harry Potter flaws to go with his strengths. Harry can be self-absorbed and insensitive to others. He also has a tendency to judge things by their appearance. "Harry is often given an erroneous first impression of someone and he has to learn to look beneath the surface," Rowling would later say in an interview. "When you look beneath the surface he has sometimes found that he is being fooled by people. And on other occasions, he has found very nice surprises."[52]

Harriett Potter

After spending several months developing her main character, Rowling suddenly faced a crisis regarding his gender. "I'd been writing about Harry for six months when I did suddenly stop and think, Hang on a moment, why is he a boy?" Rowling recalled. On a simple level, Rowling knew that she had created a male character because that was what she pictured in her mind's eye: "A boy appeared in my brain—just this little scrawny, black-haired boy with glasses on. And so I wrote him, because he was the character who came to me."[53]

Still, Rowling wondered if she would be able to create a convincing male character and sustain him over the course of seven books. As a feminist, Rowling also felt a tinge of guilt about creating another children's book with a strong male—rather than female—main character. "I did stop and think, Shouldn't it have been Harriett?" Rowling recalled. Despite her misgivings, Rowling decided not to change her book. "At that point it was too late," she said. "It was just too late, because Harry was too real to me as a boy. And Hermione was with me at this point, and I feel that Hermione is an absolutely indispensable part of the team. I love her as a character, and so I didn't change it. I wanted to go with my initial inspiration."[54]

By the end of 1990, Rowling had resolved the crisis of her main character's identity, created his inner circle of friends, and outlined the plot of her seven-book series. As elements of the story took shape, Rowling remained convinced that the concept was strong. "The idea that we could have a child who escapes from the confines of the adult world and goes somewhere where he has power, both literally and metaphorically, really appealed to me,"[55] she later said. Despite her own excitement, Rowling worried that others might not think the idea was that good. As she headed home to Tutshill for Christmas, Rowling decided that she would not yet tell anyone in her family about Harry Potter.

It was a decision she would later regret.

Chapter 3

Loss and Love

WHEN ROWLING RETURNED to Tutshill to spend the Christmas holiday with her family, her life was going reasonably well. Although she had yet to find a job to her liking, her secret career as a writer was in high gear as she pursued what she believed to be the idea of a lifetime. Her relationship with her longtime boyfriend was solid, and her small family remained close and loving. In a few short months, however, much would change. Rowling would experience losses unlike any she had known before, and these changes would send her life in a new direction.

Sadness, Guilt, and Regret

When Rowling saw her parents for the first time in many months, she was struck by her mother's frail appearance. "Her mobility was very limited; she looked ill, very ill—which I'd never really seen before," Rowling remembered. "She was absolutely exhausted."[56] About ten years earlier, Rowling's mother had been diagnosed with multiple sclerosis, a degenerative nerve disease. From the time she was fifteen, Rowling had watched her mother's health slowly decline. But because she had grown accustomed to this process, Rowling did not view the latest changes in her mother's appearance as especially alarming.

On Christmas Eve, Rowling said good-bye to her parents and left to spend the remainder of the holidays with her boyfriend. A week later, on New Year's Eve, Rowling received a call from her father at 7:30 A.M., a highly unusual occurrence. When she heard her father's voice, Rowling was filled with dread. Her fears were justified: Her father was calling to inform her that her mother had died.

The author's despair over her mother's death was reflected in the character of Harry Potter, pictured here onscreen.

Her mother's death hit Rowling hard. For one thing, Rowling was still a young woman—only twenty-five—when her mother died. She did not have a husband or children of her own to help cushion the blow. With only a twenty-year age difference between Rowling and her mother, the two had been especially close. "To me she was almost like an older sister," Rowling later explained. "I was never in any doubt that she was my mum, but that kind of relationship was there. I could talk to her a lot more freely than some of my friends spoke to their mothers."[57]

Rowling blamed herself for not noticing that her mother was near death. She felt guilty about not staying with her during her final days and about not saying a proper good-bye. "I had no idea that MS would hit her so quickly," she later admitted. "And I wasn't there. That stirs up such guilt."[58]

To escape from her sadness, Rowling turned to her writing. The world of Harry Potter did not turn out to be a refuge from her pain but a place for her to experience it in a different way. Without realizing it, Rowling put her feelings about her mother's death into her writing. Although she had made Harry Potter an orphan for practical reasons, after her mother's death, she began to write about his lost parents with greater sensitivity. She revealed that as an infant, Harry survived his encounter with Voldemort through the selfless love of his mother. In what would become the twelfth chapter of her first book, Harry looks into the Mirror of Erised ("Desire" spelled backwards) and sees his parents, alive and well, aware of who he is and what he has accomplished. "Not until I'd reread what I'd written did I realize that that had been taken entirely—entirely—from how I felt about my mother's death," Rowling later observed. "In fact, death and bereavement and what death means, I would say, is one of the central themes in all seven books."[59]

Considering how close she had been to her mother, Rowling found it odd that she never told her about Harry Potter and his magical world. "She knew I wrote, but she never read any of it," Rowling later told Elisabeth Dunn of the *Daily Telegraph*. "Can you imagine how much I regret that?"[60]

"I Wanted to Get Away"

After her mother's cremation, Rowling returned to Manchester filled with sadness. In this fragile condition, Rowling felt overwhelmed. When her job at the Chamber of Commerce suddenly ended, she took a job at the University of Manchester, but was very unhappy with her new position. Her relationship with her boyfriend also was deteriorating. In a final crushing blow, burglars broke into her home and took her most prized possessions. "We were burgled, and everything my mother had left me was stolen," Rowling recalled. "People were incredibly kind and friendly, but I decided that I wanted to get away."[61]

Not sure what she wanted to do, Rowling scanned the want ads in the *Guardian* newspaper. She came across an advertisement seeking qualified English teachers for a school located in Oporto, Portugal. Remembering the pleasant year she had spent teaching English in Paris, Rowling applied for the position.

The man who had placed the advertisement, Steve Cassidy, the principal of the Encounter English Schools in Oporto, agreed to meet with Rowling at a hotel near the railway station in Leeds. Cassidy was a bit taken aback by Rowling's appearance. "She was a bit gothic-looking with very dark eye shadow," Cassidy recalled. "She looked like Morticia from the Addams family." Despite her appearance, Rowling made a positive impression. "We had coffee and chatted," Cassidy remembered. "She wasn't an outstanding candidate, but I thought she would be OK. She was a bit shy and I remember she looked a bit sad at the station. I think her mother had recently died."[62]

Cassidy offered Rowling the position, and she accepted it. She packed a few things—including her notes on Harry Potter— and flew to Oporto in November 1991. Cassidy met Rowling at the airport and drove her to her new home, a four-bedroom apartment that she would share with two other new teachers, Aine Kiely and Jill Prewett.

Oporto

In 1991, Rowling moved to Oporto, Portugal, to teach English as a second language. The second largest city in the country, Oporto has more than 325,000 inhabitants in the city alone, 1 million in the metropolitan area, and 1.5 million in the district area. Situated on the northern bank of the Douro River where it flows into the Atlantic Ocean, Oporto has served as an important port since the Roman Empire. The city is perhaps best known for its connection to port wine, which was named after the town. This sweet, fortified red wine is aged and bottled in Oporto. Port is known around the world as a wine of remarkable character.

The city of Oporto overlooks the Douro River.

Like Rowling, Kiely and Prewett were single, in their twenties, and from the British Isles: Kiely from Ireland and Prewett from England. Besides living and working together, the three also shared a social life, visiting Oporto's numerous bars and dance clubs on a regular basis.

Passion in Oporto

On one of these outings in March 1992, the three friends ventured out to the Ribeiro, or riverside, section of the city, a beautiful area overlooking the Douro River. Rowling, Kiely, and Prewett entered a club called Meia Cava and made their way to a downstairs lounge that featured jazz music. The arrival of the three young women caught the eye of a Portuguese journalism student named Jorge Arantes. He was particularly struck by

While in Oporto, Rowling struck up an acquaintance with the man who would later become her husband.

Rowling's Celtic good looks. "This girl with the most amazing blue eyes walked in,"[63] Arantes remembered.

Fluent in English, Arantes approached the three foreigners and began to speak with Rowling. At one point, Rowling mentioned that she was rereading Jane Austen's *Sense and Sensibility,* a book that Arantes had read. The fact that Arantes could converse about Rowling's favorite author made a good impression on the young English teacher. "We were very comfortable with each other and spoke for at least two hours," Arantes recalled. "At the end of the evening we shared a kiss and exchanged phone numbers."[64]

Not wanting to appear overeager, Arantes put off calling Rowling for a couple of days. When he called, Rowling agreed to go on a date. The two again enjoyed each other's company and found they had even more in common. Soon, they had fallen in love and were seeing each other several times a week.

After a few weeks, Rowling and Arantes decided to live together. They moved in with Arantes's elderly mother, Marília Rodrigues, sharing her two-bedroom, ground-floor flat on rua Duque de Saldanha, not far from the Douro River. Rodrigues welcomed Rowling into her home. "She was a lovely woman and I saw her as part of the family,"[65] Rodrigues later said.

For the first time since her mother's death, Rowling seemed happy. Her friend Maria Inês Aguiar, the assistant director of the Encounter English School, noticed the change in her. She recalled that when Rowling first arrived in Oporto, she "was a very nervous person, anxious and whirring around like a butterfly. She had this hysterical laugh which was a bit weird. I think she wasn't fulfilled. You could see there was something missing. I think Joanne was desperate for love." Arantes gave Rowling love, and it showed in her life and work. "Jorge gave her an impetus, a release from her unhappiness,"[66] Aguiar said.

By the summer of 1992, two years after first conceiving the Potter series, Rowling had started to draft sections of what would become *Harry Potter and the Philosopher's Stone* (*Harry Potter and the Sorcerer's Stone* in the United States). She shared the beginnings of her story with Arantes, who claims to have recognized it as a masterpiece. "It was obvious to me straight away that this was the work of a genius," Arantes later told Dennis Rice of the

Daily Express. "I can still remember telling Joanne, 'Whoa! I am in love with a great, great writer.'"[67]

A Surprising Proposal

In late summer, Arantes proposed to Rowling, and she accepted. Rowling later joked about the day in a letter she wrote to Arantes: "August 28, 1992. Jorge Arantes asked Joanne Rowling to marry him, taking himself by surprise almost as much as her."[68]

On Friday, October 16, 1992, Rowling and Arantes appeared at the civil registry office in Oporto to be married. Di Rowling and her boyfriend flew in from Edinburgh, Scotland, to witness the ceremony. Within a few weeks of the wedding, Rowling found out that she was pregnant. Throughout the pregnancy, Rowling continued to teach. In her spare time, she worked on Harry Potter, sometimes venturing into nearby cafés to write. Although she lost weight during the pregnancy, Rowling gave birth to a healthy baby girl on July 27, 1993. Rowling later called the birth of her daughter "without doubt the best moment of my life."[69]

Rowling and Arantes named their baby Jessica. Rowling says that she named her daughter after Jessica Mitford. Arantes disagrees. He says that they chose the name Jessica Isabel after the biblical figure Jezebel.

The disagreement over the origins of Jessica's name is a mild example of a serious problem that existed throughout their relationship. From the beginning, Rowling and Arantes bickered often and sometimes publicly. One afternoon the couple got into an argument in the Casa Imperio, a café across the street from the school where Rowling taught. According to Maria Inês Aguiar, the fight turned physical. "He pushed her and she screamed,"[70] Aguiar recalled. Rowling ran from the café and Arantes pursued her. Rowling crossed the street, entered the school, and locked herself in a classroom. Before the argument ended, a small crowd had gathered outside the school and the police had been summoned.

Breakup

The couple's discord did not end with their marriage or with the birth of their child. In fact, the stress of coping with a newborn baby made matters worse. On November 17, 1993, the couple's frustrations erupted into the worst fight of their relationship. Arantes later said that the argument started when Rowling told him that she no longer loved him. Hurt and angry, Arantes forced Rowling out of their home. "I had to drag her out of the house at five in the morning and I admit I slapped her very hard in the street,"[71] Arantes said. He then returned to the house and locked Rowling out. Alone in the street, Rowling knew her marriage was over.

Rowling returned to the flat she had once shared with Jill Prewett and Aine Kiely and told her friends what had happened. Later that morning, the three women asked Maria Inês Aguiar to try to get four-month-old Jessica away from Arantes. Aguiar asked a friend who was a police officer to escort her to Arantes's home. Although the officer was not authorized to do anything, his presence helped persuade Arantes to give up the baby.

Reunited with Jessica, Rowling decided to leave the country. She informed Steve Cassidy of her decision, and within two weeks she boarded a plane bound for England. Aguiar believes that the diverse backgrounds of Rowling and Arantes doomed the relationship. "I don't think he and Joanne had enough time together to build a bridge between the two cultures,"[72] Aguiar explained.

After her plane touched down in London, Rowling ventured to the baggage area to collect the suitcases that contained almost everything she owned. Two years had passed since she had fled from Britain at one of the lowest points of her life. When she returned, things were even worse. She had no job, nowhere to live, and very little money. "Pretty much everything was gone," she remembered. In her arms, she held a four-month-old baby that was dependent on her for everything. Inside, Rowling felt angry—not at her estranged husband but at herself. "I never expected to find myself in that situation, and I was furious with myself," she later recalled. Still, Rowling had no regrets. "I certainly never regretted leaving, and I never ever for a second regretted Jessica," she said. "She kept me going."[73]

Chapter 4

Poverty and Perseverance

Joanne Rowling returned to Great Britain from Portugal facing a bleak future. Her marriage had collapsed and she had a baby to care for, but no money and no means of support. Just as when she found herself seated on the far right side of her fifth grade class, Rowling was discouraged, but she did not give up. Before things would get better, however, they would get worse.

Welfare Mom

Although she was glad to be back in her home country, Rowling felt out of place in London. She did not want to impose on her old friends, most of whom were single and carefree. She had enough money to rent an apartment for a couple of months, but no job prospects, and no child care for Jessica even if she found a job.

As Rowling pondered her next move, she phoned her sister, Di, who had moved to Edinburgh, Scotland. Just two months earlier, Di had married a successful restaurant owner named Roger Moore. Di suggested that Rowling come to Edinburgh and stay at her home until she found a place of her own. Rowling agreed to give Edinburgh a try. She packed her things, bought a train ticket, and headed off to Scotland.

Once in Edinburgh, Rowling decided to go on public assistance until she found a teaching position. On December 21, 1993, Rowling visited the Department of Social Security to apply for welfare. The Exeter graduate and former teacher found the process demeaning. "You have to be interviewed and explain

Edinburgh Castle sits on a cliff overlooking Edinburgh, where Rowling moved to be near her sister Di.

to a lot of strangers how you came to be penniless and the sole carer of your child," Rowling recalled. "I know that nobody was setting out to make me feel humiliated and worthless, though that is exactly how I felt."[74] Rowling's application was approved, and early in 1994 she began to receive £69 ($103.50) a week for support.

Rowling was not able to leave her feelings of shame behind at the welfare office, however; they returned every time she cashed her check. To prevent welfare fraud, the government required welfare recipients to cash their checks at a post office. Before they could get their money, however, they had to sign their names in a large book in plain view of everyone. Rowling felt embarrassed every time she went through the ordeal, especially since British prime minister John Major had criticized single-parent households in a speech in October 1993. "I don't know what all the old ladies behind me would say if they saw it—'scrounger', 'layabout' and 'burden on society,'" Rowling remembered thinking.

With no job and a small child to support, Rowling had little choice but to endure the humiliation. "By this time most of the pride had been squashed out of me,"[75] she recalled.

Rowling Hits Bottom

Rowling rented one of the very few apartments she could afford. Not long after moving in, she discovered that she and Jessica were not alone in the flat: A family of mice was living in the walls. Rowling again felt angry. "I never expected to mess up so badly that I would find myself in . . . [a] mouse-infested flat, looking after my daughter," she remembered. "And I was angry because I felt I was letting her down."[76]

Rowling wanted to work her way out of her crummy apartment, but she found herself stuck in what she called "an appalling poverty trap."[77] She could not get a job unless she had child care for Jessica, but she could not afford child care without

With the help of her friend Sean Harris, Rowling moved from a mouse-infested apartment to a flat in Leith (pictured), the old port area of Edinburgh.

a job. The government offered child care programs but only for children deemed "at risk." Rowling's application was turned down because she was taking good care of Jessica.

Unable to afford to move to another place, Rowling appealed to longtime friend Sean Harris for help. Luckily, Harris came to the rescue. He gave Rowling the money she needed to move into a one-bedroom flat in Leith, the old port area of Edinburgh. Di and a few friends lent Rowling some furniture, and she began to settle in at 7 South Lorne Place.

Rowling was glad to have a better place for her and Jessica to live, but she was still lonely and depressed. To escape the solitude, she once visited a friend of her sister's who had a baby boy named Thomas. The visit turned into a nightmare. "I saw Thomas's bedroom full of toys and at that point, when I packed Jessica's toys away, they fitted into a shoe box, literally," Rowling recalled. Ashamed that she could not provide more playthings for her daughter, Rowling broke down. "I came home and cried my eyes out,"[78] she said.

The Turning Point

For comfort during these difficult times, Rowling often turned to her younger sister. Di had always been a cheerful person who loved to laugh, and her good spirits gave her more melancholy sister a lift. During one visit, Rowling mentioned that she was working on a new book. Just as when they were little, Di wanted to hear all about the story. Rowling agreed to let Di read the three chapters she had completed. Emotionally fragile, Rowling sensed that she probably would not have the strength to finish the book if it failed to entertain her kid sister. For a few minutes, the only sound in the room was the faint rustle of paper as Di turned the pages. Finally, a smile crept across her face and she laughed out loud. "It's possible that if she hadn't laughed, I would have set the whole thing on one side [abandoned the project],"[79] Rowling later said.

Encouraged by Di's reaction, Rowling decided to do whatever it would take to finish the novel. After completing it, she would go back to work full-time. If nothing came of the book, she at least would know that she had seen the project through.

Rowling found that writing while Jessica was awake was nearly impossible. To be productive, she devised a special writing routine:

> I had to make full use of all the time that my then-baby daughter slept. This meant writing in the evenings and during nap times. I used to put her into the pushchair and walk her around Edinburgh, wait until she nodded off, and then hurry to a café and write as fast as I could. It's amazing how much you can get done when you know you have very limited time. I've probably never been as productive since, if you judge by words per hour.[80]

One of her favorite places to write was Nicolson's Café, an establishment co-owned by Rowling's brother-in-law, Roger Moore. With yellow and blue cloths covering the tables and prints by the French artist Henri Matisse dotting the walls, Nicolson's had a Bohemian atmosphere that appealed to Rowling. "She was quite often in several times a week, a good few hours at a time," Moore recalled. "She was quite an odd sight," remembered Dougal McBride, Moore's business partner. "She would just push the pram [baby carriage] with one hand and write away."[81]

As she worked, Rowling gave herself over to the story without concerning herself about who would read it or how it would be marketed. "I wasn't really aware that it was a children's book," she later said. "I really wrote it for me, about what I found funny, what I liked."[82]

Divorce

Just as Rowling was settling into a stable writing routine, she received word that her estranged husband had shown up in town, looking for her and Jessica. Remembering how badly Arantes had treated her in Oporto, Rowling filed papers on March 15, 1994, to obtain a type of restraining order, known as an action of interdict, against him. The court granted Rowling an interim order that prevented Arantes "from molesting, abusing her verbally, threatening her or putting her in a state of fear and alarm by using violence towards her anywhere within the sheriffdom of Edinburgh."[83] Barred from seeing his wife and daughter,

Arantes left the country. Her husband's appearance in Edinburgh was enough to convince Rowling to file for divorce, which she did on August 10, 1994. In November 1994, she renewed the interdict against Arantes, just in case he returned. At home in Portugal, Arantes did not challenge these proceedings, so on June 26, 1995, the interdict became permanent. That same day, their divorce became final.

After Arantes returned to Portugal, Rowling returned to the world of Harry Potter. "The book . . . saved my sanity, it truly did," she later said. "I wrote furiously while my daughter slept, which not only gave me something to do with my brain but was an escape for me, too."[84]

A Superhuman Effort

By the end of 1994, the end of the book was in sight, and Rowling began to make plans for what she would do after she finished the book. She discovered that her degree from Exeter and her teaching experience did not qualify her to teach foreign language in Scotland. To register with the General Teaching Council in Scotland, Rowling needed a postgraduate certificate of education (PGCE). To obtain the teaching credential, she had to complete a yearlong program that included both course work and a stint as a student teacher. In January 1995, Rowling applied for one of the thirty openings in a program at Heriot-Watt University that would begin that August. After completing a daylong interview conducted in French, the subject she had applied to teach, Rowling was accepted into the program.

To support herself as a full-time student, Rowling applied for a grant from the Scottish Office of Education and Industry. Contrary to later reports, it was this grant, not the one she would receive from the Scottish Arts Council a year later, that supported Rowling as she completed her first book. With money from the grant and the financial assistance of a friend she has never named, Rowling went off welfare in the summer of 1995.

As the starting date of her schooling approached, Rowling hurried to complete her book. "I knew that unless I made a push to finish the first book now, I might never finish it," Rowling recalled. "I made a huge, superhuman effort."[85] By the time

After five years of intense work on her first Harry Potter book, Rowling was ready at last to send the book to prospective publishers.

school began, Rowling had finished a rough draft of the book, but she continued to polish the manuscript. Late in 1995, she began to type the manuscript on a secondhand manual typewriter. With little money to spend on photocopies, Rowling decided to type out two complete copies of the manuscript to submit to publishers.

Not sure what to do next, Rowling visited the Edinburgh Central Library and looked through a copy of *Writers' & Artists' Yearbook* to find publishers and authors' agents that might be interested in what she called her "quirky little book."[86] As she pored over the list of agents, one name stood out to the lover of unusual names: the Christopher Little Literary Agency in Walham Grove, Fulham.

An Interested Reader

On the surface, Rowling did not choose wisely: the Christopher Little Agency did not represent children's authors. Accordingly, when Rowling's manuscript arrived at the agency on a cold February morning in 1996, Little's personal assistant and office manager, Bryony Evens, placed *Harry Potter and the Philosopher's Stone* in the pile to be returned. "There would be no point in showing it to Chris if we didn't deal with it anyway,"[87] Evens later explained.

However, Evens was not the typical manuscript screener. Just twenty-five years old and on the job less than two years, Evens had a youthful curiosity about the books submitted to the agency, and she often glanced through the rejected submissions before returning them. The day that Rowling's manuscript arrived, Evens spent her lunch hour picking through the day's submissions. She lingered over Rowling's manuscript, examining the drawings the author had included with her work. "The first thing I noticed was that there were illustrations with it," Evens recalled. "There was one of Harry standing by the fireplace in the Dursley's house with his scruffy hair and the lightning scar on his forehead."[88]

Intrigued by the artwork, Evens turned to page one. A devoted fan of *Lord of the Rings* and other tales of fantasy and adventure, Evens liked what she saw. "I read the first page and thought it was really good,"[89] she recalled.

Instead of mailing the sample chapters back to Rowling, Evens set the manuscript aside to read later. When she returned to the manuscript later in the day, she was even more impressed. "The main thing that struck me, because I loved it, was the humor,"[90] Evens remembered. Even though it was not her job to discover authors, Evens decided to approach Christopher Little with the manuscript. Impressed by her enthusiasm, Little agreed to let Evens request the complete manuscript.

"I Could Not Believe It"

When Rowling found a letter from the Christopher Little Literary Agency in her mailbox, she was not particularly excited. She had already received a rejection note from one literary agency and one publisher. She braced herself for another. "I assumed it was a rejection note," she recalled, "but inside the envelope there was a letter saying, 'Thank you. We would be pleased to receive the balance of your manuscript on an exclusive basis.'" Six long years had passed since Harry Potter had first appeared in Rowling's imagination. She had spent countless hours developing his personality, creating his friends and enemies, and devising dangers and narrow escapes. Now, for the first time, someone outside her family was showing an interest in his world. "I could not believe it," she later said. "I read it eight times."[91]

Rowling sent the remainder of the book to Christopher Little immediately. Sorting through the mail, Evens was the first to see the complete manuscript. "When it came I just couldn't put it down," she remembered.

> I had already decided that, even if we had rejected it, I was going to read the rest of it for my own curiosity. I remember making a mental list of what was great about it —it had a school story, the orphan with an evil stepfamily, lots of witches, wizards, a really good detective story with a twist at the end of the story. And there was nothing that had made me laugh as much on first reading since Diana Wynne Jones' "Charmed Life" in the 1970's.[92]

After reading the manuscript, Evens gave it to Little with the highest possible recommendation. When Little left the office that evening, he took the manuscript with him. Later that night, he read the hand-typed pages that would change his life. The next morning, he returned to the office filled with enthusiasm. He congratulated Evens on her find, and the two discussed what to do next. They agreed that they would ask Rowling to make minor revisions. "We made a list of the things we thought weren't quite strong enough," Evens said. "I thought there should be more of Neville, and Christopher wanted to know more about Quidditch," Evens recalled. "But there was hardly anything else."[93]

A Contract at Last

Rowling was not put off by the agent's suggestions. On the contrary, she was delighted with them. "Rowling wrote back saying, that's brilliant because I like Neville,"[94] Evens remembered. She had also already created the rules to Quidditch, but had taken

While making revisions to her manuscript, Rowling never envisioned crowds like this one lining up for autographed copies of her book.

them out of the final draft of the manuscript because she thought they were too detailed. She gladly put them back in. When she mailed back her revisions, Rowling even enclosed an illustration of a Quidditch match.

After a few additional changes, Evens showed the manuscript to Patrick Walsh, Christopher Little's business partner. Walsh agreed that the agency should offer Rowling a contract to represent her. Little sent Rowling a standard contract, binding her exclusively to the agency for five years, an arrangement that could be renewed on a year-to-year basis. In exchange for representing Rowling to publishers, filmmakers, and merchandising companies, the agency would receive 15 percent of the book earnings in the United Kingdom and 20 percent of the film and international earnings. Rowling accepted the contract without hesitation.

The Search for a Publisher

With the contract secured, Little put Evens in charge of shopping the manuscript around to various publishers. To avoid spending

Joanne, Jo, Jake

When J.K. Rowling was growing up, her teachers called her Joanne, but her friends and family knew her simply as Jo. For professional purposes, she went by her full name, Joanne Rowling. This was the name she typed on the manuscript of *Harry Potter and the Philosopher's Stone* and at the bottom of her letter to the Christopher Little Literary Agency.

When Rowling's first book was accepted for publication, Christopher Little insisted that she replace her first name with her initials to keep her gender a secret. Little had heard that, although girls were willing to read books by male authors, boys tended to shun books by female authors. Rowling agreed to the scheme, but everyone felt that J. Rowling sounded too plain. Rowling thought of adding the initial K., which would stand for her grandmother's name, Kathleen. When Rowling's close friends heard about the pen name, they teased her by calling her Jake.

Once *Harry Potter and the Philosopher's Stone* became a hit, Rowling's publicity agents told the press that J.K. stood for Joanne Kathleen. The publication of Rowling's birth certificate by a Bristol newspaper in July 2000 caused a minor furor over the author's real name. Richard Savill of the *Telegraph* wrote, "The author of the Harry Potter books has performed her own personal conjuring trick. Joanne Rowling, better known by her initials J K, does not have a middle name, according to her birth certificate. The use of the author's initials instead of her full name was a marketing ploy designed to make her work acceptable to boys, who actively choose not to read books by women." Reacting to the news story, a spokesperson for Bloomsbury in that same article said, "Clearly it was not her name given at birth but it could have been her confirmation name. When we asked her for her initials, she said J K."

According to that same article, Rowling later explained to an interviewer, "It was the publisher's idea, they could have called me Enid Snodgrass. I just wanted it [the book] published."

too much money promoting a book by an unknown author, Little asked Evens to make just three photocopies of the two-hundred-page manuscript. One by one, the first three submissions were returned. As the manuscripts came back, Evens sent them out to other publishers. A total of twelve publishers passed on the opportunity to publish *Harry Potter and the Philosopher's Stone* before Evens slipped the manuscript into an envelope addressed to Bloomsbury Publishing, which had just created a children's book division.

Barry Cunningham, who headed the new division, was the first person at Bloomsbury to read Rowling's manuscript. "It was just terribly exciting," Cunningham remembered. "What struck me first was that the book came with a fully imagined world. There was a complete sense of Jo knowing the characters and what would happen to them."[95]

Cunningham showed the book to three other members of his staff: Janet Hogart, Eleanor Bagenal, and Rosamund de la Hay. Each of them liked it. "It made me laugh out loud and stay up all night reading it,"[96] de la Hay recalled.

Before Cunningham and his associates could offer Rowling a contract, they had to gain the support of the company directors, few of whom paid much attention to the children's book division. De la Hay suggested that Cunningham attach a package of Smarties candies to copies of the manuscript before sending them around—a not-so-subtle hint that the book might earn the Smarties Prize, one of Britain's most prestigious awards for children's literature. The gimmick worked. The directors authorized Cunningham to offer Rowling a £1,500 ($2,250) advance against royalties for the right to publish the book.

Christopher Little called his client to give her the good news. Rowling was thrilled beyond words. "I jumped and touched the ceiling of my living room,"[97] she later recalled. For the lover of books who had been writing stories since the age of six, who had started and abandoned two novels, and who had spent six long years bringing a momentary vision to life, the news of impending publication was a dream come true:

> It sounds a bit twee [excessively dainty or quaint], but nothing since has matched the moment when I actually realized that "Harry" was going to be published. That was the realization of my life's ambition—to be a published author—and the culmination of so much effort on my part. The mere fact that I would see my book on a bookshelf in a bookshop made me happier than I can say.[98]

Chapter 5

"The Pinnacle of Achievement"

IN 1997, 102,925 BOOKS were published in the United Kingdom. The chances of any one of them becoming a best-seller were practically nil, least of all, perhaps, a children's book by an unknown writer with an initial hardcover print run of just five hundred copies. No one was more aware of this fact than the author of such a small-run children's book, Joanne Rowling. "I had been very realistic about the likelihood of making a living out of writing children's books—I knew it was exceptionally rare for anybody to do it—and that didn't worry me," she remembered. "I prayed that I would make just enough money to justify continuing to write, because I am supporting my daughter single-handedly."[99] Her prayers would be answered. Within a month of its publication, Rowling's first book would become one of the best-selling books in the United Kingdom.

Success would not come overnight, however. In fact, it took more than a year from the time her book was accepted by Bloomsbury until it appeared in her local bookshop. In the meantime, Rowling had to support herself and her daughter and somehow make time to continue telling the story of Harry Potter and his Hogwarts friends.

Becoming a Teacher

Rowling was scheduled to receive her advance from Bloomsbury in two payments—one half after signing the contract and the other half after the book was published. After the Christopher Little Literary Agency took its 15 percent out of the

54

Rowling's success was slow in coming, but her best-selling books would eventually appear in bookstores around the world. Here a bookstore manager arranges a display of Harry Potter products.

advance, Rowling received just £637.50 ($955) for the first payment—a nice addition to her bank account, but not enough to change her life. She continued to live at South Lorne Place and pursue her teaching certificate.

Rowling was in the midst of her student teaching assignment when she received word that her book would be published. Although she took teaching seriously, she received low marks at the beginning of her term. Her tutor, Michael Lynch, gave her D grades in lesson content and class management; Cs in communication, methodology, knowledge of the school, and assessment; and a borderline B in professionalism. Rowling worked hard to improve her performance in the classroom. In his second assessment, Lynch gave her Bs in all areas except knowledge of the school. By the end of the summer session, Rowling had raised her grades even higher. Her new tutor, Eliane Whitelaw, gave Rowling straight As. "She had some of my classes and she was very good," Whitelaw recalled. "She was very organized and professional but also had a very good relationship with the kids. She was a very good person in the classroom."[100]

Rowling used her creative skills in her teaching just as she did in her writing. She devised a card game designed to help her students make simple sentences in French. Each card contained a word and an illustration. The cards were placed in two equal piles. To play, the student drew one card from each pile and attempted to make a sentence using the words on the cards. If the student succeeded, he or she could keep the cards. If not, the cards were placed at the bottoms of the piles. "Joanne was very imaginative," remembered Richard Easton, another of Rowling's tutors. "I believe that's the most important quality a teacher can have. Some people teach from the textbook and that will be that, whereas somebody who has a bit of creative flair

Leith Academy

After she was awarded her teaching credential, J.K. Rowling briefly taught at Leith Academy in Edinburgh. The following account of the school's history comes from its website.

Leith Academy is one of the oldest schools in Scotland. Its usual date of founding is given as 1560, but there are references to the "grammer scule of Leith" as early as 1521. In 1560 Leith Grammar School was placed under the Control of the Kirk Session of Leith Parish, and remained there until 1806.

During its first years, there is no information as to where the school was sited. However, in 1636 the school is mentioned as meeting in Trinity House, where, apart from a few years when Cromwell's army used Trinity House for stores, it stayed until 1710.

After disagreements about the rent for Trinity House (£3 per year) the Kirk Session moved the school to the King James' Hospital, which stood within the present ground of South Leith Churchyard. But by 1792, the school was "damp, confined, and otherwise unhealthy for boys". Following such protest from the local people, the Kirk Session agreed to build the new Leith High School on Leith Links. Public subscriptions raised almost £3000 and the new school was completed in 1806.

This building served the students of Leith for many years, changing its name to Leith Academy in 1888. But the increasing numbers of students finally resulted in the building of Leith Academy in Duke Street in 1931. The building remains as Leith Primary School.

The Leith Academy we know today was opened in May 1991, following a long campaign by parents, students and staff.

can come up with all sorts of interesting games. I remember Joanne's drawings. She was using her own skills and making them useful as a teaching material."[101]

Rowling graduated from the PGCE program in July 1996 and registered as a supply, or substitute, teacher with the General Teaching Council. In another sign that her fortunes were changing, Rowling landed a part-time teaching job at Leith Academy, a school located just six hundred yards from her front door. Founded in 1560, Leith Academy is one of the oldest schools in Scotland. The current campus, which opened in May 1991, is a modern structure of steel, glass, and brick that resembles a cross between an arboretum and Hogwarts School of Witchcraft and Wizardry—a light-filled maze of hallways and classrooms dotted with indoor plants and trees. Best of all for Rowling, the school housed an onsite day care center where she could leave Jessica while she taught.

"Miss, Are You a Writer?"

Among the teachers at Leith was Eliane Whitelaw, who tutored Rowling when she was a student teacher. Rowling and Whitelaw became friends, meeting for coffee outside school from time to time. Rowling told Whitelaw about the upcoming publication of her book, but otherwise she kept her writing career a secret. The news almost got out when Rowling sent one of her students to her desk to get some paper. "She was ages at the desk," Rowling later told the *Guardian*, "and I turned round and said, 'Maggie will you come back and sit down,' and she went 'Miss, are you a writer?' I think I said, 'No it's just a hobby.'"[102]

It was about to become much more than that. Rowling applied for a writer's grant from the Scottish Arts Council to help supplement her income. Only residents of Scotland who had already published a book were eligible to apply for the grant. Although Rowling's first book was not yet out, the council agreed to consider her proposal. "We decided that Joanne would be eligible because she already had a contract with Bloomsbury," explained the council's literary director, Jenny Brown. "She wanted the grant to help her while she wrote the second Harry Potter book."[103] After reading a few chapters of *Harry Potter and the Philosopher's*

Scottish Arts Council Awards

In February 1997, the Scottish Arts Council (SAC) awarded the unknown author Joanne Rowling a grant of £8,000 ($12,000) so that
she could continue work on her second novel, *Harry Potter and the
Chamber of Secrets*. In a news release on the Scottish Arts Council
website, SAC literature director Jenny Brown uses Rowling's success
to illustrate how awards of this nature play an important role in the
continuing support of the arts.

> This is a small budget programme that can make a real differ-
> ence to writers who are struggling financially. It can give them
> the financial freedom they need, often for a relatively short pe-
> riod of time, to do what they want to do most in the world and
> that is to write. We have seen with the example of J.K. Rowl-
> ing, that a relatively small amount of money, in Joanne Rowl-
> ing's case £8,000, can make the difference between being
> unable to finish a work because of lack of funding and submit-
> ting a completed manuscript to a publisher.

Stone, Brown recommended Rowling as one of forty finalists for
the ten awards. On the strength of her application, the council
awarded Rowling the largest of its ten grants, £8,000 ($12,000)—
more than five times as much as her advance from Bloomsbury.

The first thing Rowling did after she received her grant was
buy a word processor so that she could revise her manuscripts
as she typed. The word processor did not change her method of
composition, however. She continued her long-held practice of
drafting her books in longhand.

Since she had created plots and sketched scenes for her second book even before she began writing her first, Rowling progressed quickly through *Harry Potter and the Chamber of Secrets*.
With the help of her word processor, Rowling shipped her second manuscript off to Christopher Little in July 1997, just a week
after her first book came off the press.

In Print at Last

Rowling once said that her "wildest fantasies hadn't gone much
further than the book being published and the pinnacle of
achievement seemed to me to be a review in a quality newspaper."[104] Rowling realized the first of her lifelong ambitions on

June 26, 1997, when Bloomsbury published the first edition of *Harry Potter and the Philosopher's Stone.*

When Rowling received the first copy of her book, she felt giddy with pride. "I walked around all day with a finished copy tucked under my arm," she told biographer Lindsey Fraser. "The first time I saw it in a bookshop I had this mad desire to sign it. It was an extraordinary moment." [105]

Not long after achieving her first goal, Rowling attained her second. A short review appeared in the *Scotsman* that hailed *Harry Potter and the Philosopher's Stone* for making "an unassailable stand for the power of fresh, innovative story-telling in the face of formula horror and sickly romance." [106]

Two weeks after the book appeared, Nicolette Jones, a reviewer for the *Sunday Times,* also praised Rowling's work:

> Not yet as well known as [authors] Philip Ridley or Robert Swindells, but surely destined to be, is J K Rowling, whose first children's book, *Harry [Potter] and the Philosopher's Stone,* is already winning accolades and

Bryony Evens Meets J.K. Rowling

While working as Christopher Little's personal assistant, Bryony Evens was the first person to spot the potential of *Harry Potter and the Philosopher's Stone.* In her article "Harry Potter's Novel Encounter," reporter Anjana Ahuja of the *London Times* described the first meeting between Evens and Rowling.

> Evens pulls a Harry Potter book from her bag and hands it to me, beaming. On an inside page is an extravagant, diagonal scrawl in black ink: "To Bryony—who is the most important person I've ever met in a signing queue & the first person ever to see merit in Harry Potter. With huge thanks. J.K. Rowling."
>
> The "huge" has been underlined four times, signifying the contribution that Evens has made to this particular phenomenon. . . .
>
> She finally met Joanne Rowling in 1998—in the signing queue at the Cheltenham Literary Festival. "My aunt got tickets and we had borrowed two children so we didn't look out of place," Evens recalls. "Then afterwards, during the signing, I told her who I was and she jumped up and gave me a hug in front of all these children."

prizes. In this very funny, imaginative, magical story, for anyone from 10 to adulthood, Harry Potter is deposited as a baby with dreadfully dull and unkind relatives, for his own protection: he is the child of heroes of the wizard world. On his 11th birthday, wizards come to claim him and train him for his destiny. This is a story full of surprises and jokes; comparisons with [children's author Roald] Dahl are, this time, justified.[107]

With reviews like that, Rowling had achieved everything she had set out to do. Anything more, she would later say, would be "gravy."

An Auction

Three days after *Harry Potter and the Philosopher's Stone* was published, Rowling's gravy boat came in. Unbeknown to the first-time author, the foreign rights for her book were being auctioned at a book fair in Bologna, Italy. At around eight in the evening, Christopher Little called to tell Rowling what was happening. He said that the bidding had reached $10,000 for the U.S. publishing rights. "They were up to five figures," Rowling recalled. "I went cold with shock."[108]

Little did Rowling know that the bidding had just begun. Arthur A. Levine, an editorial director at Scholastic, was prepared to go much higher than $10,000. He had been introduced to *Harry Potter and the Philosopher's Stone* by Janet Hogart, who had left Bloomsbury to work for Scholastic, and had read the book on his plane ride from New York to Bologna. "The thing I loved the most about reading *Harry Potter* is the idea of growing up unappreciated, feeling outcast and then this great satisfaction of being discovered," Levine later wrote. "That is the fantasy of every person who grows up feeling marginalized in any way. Along with the imagination and the wonderful writing, that's the emotional connection that drew me to the book."[109] Levine decided that the book had all the qualities of a classic, and he would treat it as such.

As the bidding climbed toward the $50,000 mark, however, Levine began to wonder if he should drop out:

Rowling was stunned that the U.S. rights for her first book in the Harry Potter series were auctioned off for the huge sum of $105,000.

It's a scary thing when you keep bidding and the stakes get higher and higher. I was getting a tremendous amount of support from my company. And that's a wonderful thing, but it's a great risk. If people believe in you and you flop, then you walk out on the plank and plunge.

It's one thing to say I love this first novel by this unknown woman in Scotland and I want to publish it. And it's another thing as the bidding goes higher. Do you love it this much? Do you love it at $50,000? At $70,000?[110]

Levine decided that he did. One bidder offered $100,000 for the rights, but Levine would not back down. He bid $105,000. It was enough. "I had never paid so much for an acquisition before," Levine recalled. He was strengthened, he said, by something he had read on his plane trip to Bologna: "In *Harry Potter,* the wand chooses the wizard; and when the wand chooses you, you take it."[111]

"Shock"

When the bidding was over, Levine wanted to talk to Rowling. "My first reaction was to call the author, J.K. Rowling, to tell her not to be frightened because I knew it would be a tremendous amount of pressure on her," he remembered. "I called her very late, and we had a very nice conversation—our first."[112]

Rowling could scarcely believe what she was being told. "My reaction was shock," Rowling remembered. "This was like being catapulted into fairyland."[113]

Levine tried to help Rowling cope with the startling news. "I said don't be scared, and she said, 'Thanks; I am,'" Levine recalled. To help Scholastic recoup the large advance, Levine knew that he would need Rowling to help promote the book. "We both said now that we've paid this much we've got to concentrate on making the book work,"[114] Levine recalled.

Rowling appreciated Levine's concern, but it hardly helped her cope with the changes she knew the windfall would bring. "He really knew what I was going through," she remembered. "I went to bed and couldn't sleep. On one level I was obviously delighted, but most of me froze."[115]

A Great News Story

Of all the things that Levine and Rowling might have thought of to make the book work, none would have the impact of what Levine already had done: By bidding the largest sum ever paid to a first-time children's author, Levine drew far more attention to Rowling than the shrewdest public relations campaign ever could have. "A penniless and newly-divorced mother has sold her first book for £100,000,"[116] blared the *Daily Mail,* just one of several newspapers that picked up the news from Bologna. With her £8,000 grant from the Scottish Arts Council tucked away in her bank account, Rowling was hardly penniless, nor did she receive the £100,000 the *Daily Mail* reported. Levine's $105,000 bid translated into about £66,000. Furthermore, Rowling had been divorced for two years. Still, Rowling's rags-to-riches story proved irresistible.

The same weekend that Scholastic bought the U.S. rights, the *Sunday Times* ran a thousand-word feature story on Rowling. Reporter Eddie Gibb dutifully played up the Cinderella story:

> The unemployed single mother lives with her toddler in a bedsit [one-room apartment] because that is all she can

A warehouse worker at the Scholastic distribution center checks book orders as boxes of Harry Potter volumes await shipment.

afford on benefit. Though she would dearly love to find a job, the cost of a nursery place would wipe out any extra income she earned. She thinks she will go mad if something does not change soon.

Joanne Rowling is both a children's author and a single mother, and until recently her life was more bedsit than country kitchen. But something has changed: her first book has just been published. The word from the British book trade on *Harry Potter and the Philosopher's Stone* is extremely positive and Scholastic, the American publishing house, has just bought the rights for a sum Rowling admits is north of $100,000 (some sources say it could be as high as $500,000). This is a handsome advance for any first novel but unheard of for a children's author.[117]

Although the sum Rowling really was paid certainly was re-markable enough, Gibb could not resist speculating that the fig-ure was five times larger than it actually was.

Meeting the Press

The Bloomsbury public relations department noted the media's curiosity about Rowling and immediately tried to make the most of it. Bloomsbury quickly arranged for an interview with Nigel Reynolds, the arts correspondent for the *Daily Telegraph*. "A young author has sold her first book to an American publisher for more than £100,000," Reynolds began. "What makes the deal remarkable is that Joanne Rowling's tome is not a novel or a heavyweight biography, but a children's story." [118] The article included a photograph of Rowling taken in a café. Ten days after her book was published, Rowling was on the third page of Britain's largest selling broadsheet newspaper.

After the interview, Reynolds reflected on his meeting with Rowling. He found her to be "a little bit anxious" about all the attention she was getting. "I told her that if all goes well then she would find her life becoming public property," Reynolds re-membered. "She seemed as though she was worried about that. She was rather stern and worried." [119]

She had reason to be. The press could not get enough of Rowling, and she wanted to give her book whatever boost she could—at almost any cost. Less than three weeks later, Rowling agreed to meet Helena de Bertodano for an even longer inter-view for the *Telegraph*. Through a series of mishaps, Rowling was an hour late. "'I'm so sorry. I'm just really really sorry,' she keeps saying, shaking like a leaf and looking as though she might cry," Bertodano wrote. Rowling had indeed been crying. "I was halfway here in the taxi and I was so upset by being so late for you, and then I realized I didn't have my purse. So I just burst into tears," [120] Rowling told the reporter.

All of the publicity spurred sales of the book. *Harry Potter and the Philosopher's Stone* entered the Booktrack best-seller list in the summer of 1997 and stayed there throughout the year. By the end of its first year, the book had sold more than seventy thousand copies in the United Kingdom alone. Meanwhile, in

Rowling meets with the press. After her first book was published, journalists were eager for stories about her personal life.

the United States, Scholastic planned an initial print run of another fifty thousand copies.

The success of the book had to do with much more than publicity, of course. The story itself was almost universally acclaimed. In November 1997, *Harry Potter and the Philosopher's Stone* received the Smarties Prize, just as Barry Cunningham and Rosamund de la Hay had predicted. It also claimed the Federation of Children's Books Group Award and was named the British Book Awards Children's Book of the Year. The woman who claimed she would never be famous was quickly becoming just that.

Little did she know that it was only the beginning.

Chapter 6

Pottermania

As her thirty-first birthday approached in the summer of 1996, J.K. Rowling, as she was becoming known to the world, was pretty well prepared to handle life's ups and downs. She had equipped herself with a good education, traveled and lived abroad, been married and divorced, given birth to a child, and lost a parent. She had struggled through grim poverty and realized a lifelong dream of publishing a book. Yet nothing could have prepared her for what was about to happen. Within five years she would become one of the richest and most recognizable women in the world. The media would report on her every move. Thousands of children would wait in line just to get a glimpse of her. Millions more would decorate their rooms with images from her books, dress up like her characters, chat about her and with her on the Internet, and go to see movies based on her work. Most important, hundreds of millions of people—children and adults alike—would read and reread her books, many experiencing the magic of literature for the first time. Through it all, Rowling would have to maintain some kind of balance in her life if she was to achieve her ultimate goal:

> I want to finish these seven books and look back and think that whatever happened—however much this hurricane whirled around me—I stayed true to what I wanted to write. This is my Holy Grail: that when I finish writing book seven, I can say—hand on heart—I didn't change a thing. I wrote the story I meant to write. If I lost readers along the way, so be it, but I still told my story. The one I wanted. Without permitting it

Rowling autographs copies of her book for two young fans. Millions of readers of every age would soon be devouring her books.

to sound too corny, that's what I owe to my characters. That we won't be deflected, either by adoration or by criticism. [121]

A New Home

Maintaining stability would not be easy, however. No sooner had she given her first interview about her first book than she began to have doubts about her second, titled *Harry Potter and the Chamber of Secrets,* which she had already turned over to her publisher. Within a week of handing in the manuscript, Rowling asked her publisher to give it back so she could make some minor changes. She kept the book for another six weeks. "I've only suffered writer's block badly once, and that was during the writing of *Chamber of Secrets,*" she later confessed. "I had my first burst of publicity about the first book, and it paralyzed me. I was scared the second book wouldn't measure up, but I got through it!" [122] Satisfied at last that the second book was as good as she could make it, Rowling returned the manuscript to her publisher and almost immediately began work on the third book of the series, *Harry Potter and the Prisoner of Azkaban.*

With the advance from Scholastic, Rowling decided to move out of her flat in Leith. Since she did not drive, she looked for a place within walking distance of her sister's home. She also wanted to be near a good primary school for Jessica to attend. Rowling found an apartment for sale near Craiglockhart Primary School on Hazelbank Terrace, a cul-de-sac with lots of families living on it. The new apartment had a sitting room, a kitchen, two bedrooms, and a converted attic space. For the first time, Jessica had a bedroom of her own and Rowling had an office.

Gradually, Rowling began to enjoy the comfort and security that her new career was bringing her. She no longer had to worry about Jessica outgrowing her clothes or shoes before she could afford new ones. Concerned that the money might not last, however, Rowling continued to watch her budget carefully. "If you have been through three or four years of worrying on a daily basis about the money running out, you are never going to forget what that's like."[123]

Harry Travels Well

Rowling had little to fear. When *Harry Potter and the Chamber of Secrets* was released in July 1998, it debuted as the top-selling book in the United Kingdom, nudging aside books by adult novelists John Grisham, Tom Clancy, and Jeffrey Archer. A month later, Scholastic released *Harry Potter and the Sorcerer's Stone* in the United States. Within four weeks, the book had flown to the top of *Publisher's Weekly*'s list of best-selling children's fiction. By mid-December, online retailer Amazon.com reported that *Harry Potter and the Sorcerer's Stone* was its second best-selling book. To satisfy demand, Scholastic went back to press seven times, each time with larger print runs. By the end of December, more than 190,000 copies were in print in the United States.

Newsweek acknowledged the book's American success. "A dark British kids' book bewitches U.S.," ran the headline. Reporter Carla Power wrote, "As melancholy as it is fantastic, 'Harry Potter' has been likened to the dark juvenile novels of

Roald Dahl and C.S. Lewis." Noting the success of the book's sequel in the United Kingdom, the reporter declared, "It's clear that the author is no one-shot wonder."[124]

Power was right. As soon as some American fans heard that the sequel to *Harry Potter and the Sorcerer's Stone* was already available in the United Kingdom, they began to order it from the British subsidiary of Amazon.com. Scholastic had planned to release *Harry Potter and the Chamber of Secrets* in September, but seeing potential orders slipping through the World Wide Web, it rushed to get the book into print. Meanwhile, *Time* fed the growing frenzy with an article that praised Rowling for conjuring up "a magical, self-contained parallel universe" that is "filled not only with characters familiar to most kids but also with clever jokes about garden gnomes and wizard chess—played with living pieces." Reporter Elizabeth Gleick concluded, "The *Wizard of Oz* just may have to make a little space on the shelf for the wizards of Hogwarts."[125]

Rowling herself was mystified by the American response. After all, the books contain no American characters or locations, and many of the details in the books—such as the foods served at Hogwarts—are peculiarly British. The same could be said for Rowling's dry sense of humor. Although Rowling professed to have no explanation for the books' popularity in the United States, she may have summed it up best when she told an interviewer for *Time*, "If it's a good book, anyone will read it."[126]

"An Absolute Tidal Wave"

Scholastic finally released *Harry Potter and the Chamber of Secrets* in June 1999. One month later, more than 900,000 copies were in print in the United States. By then, more than 860,000 copies of *Harry Potter and the Sorcerer's Stone* also were in print. Both books landed on the *New York Times* best-seller list. The series had been translated into twenty-five languages and was being sold in 115 countries. Five million copies of the books were in print worldwide. Rowling's royalty checks, which were paid every six months, finally began to reflect the boom in sales. That summer, Rowling received her first £1 million ($1.5 million) royalty check.

Rowling Splurges

Even after J.K. Rowling began to earn a great deal of money from her books, she was very careful about how she spent it. That all changed one day shortly after her ex-husband sold his story to a British newspaper. Simon Hattenstone of the *Guardian* told the story in his article "Harry, Jessie and Me."

> I ask her what is the most extravagant thing she has done with all her millions. She says it came at a time when she was struggling with the plot to book four, just after Jorge's story of their marriage was published. She was sitting in her favourite writing cafe, had been there two hours, and the paper was blank with self-pity. "I was just feeling very down, and really worried about the book, and then I thought there is an upside to this situation and I walked into this jeweller's and I dropped a lot of money on a very expensive ring that I'd seen the previous week. And you know when you spend more money than you plan to, everything else looks cheap by comparison—so then I bought presents for my two best female friends as well. And I have to say it helped."
>
> Where's the ring now? "At home." What's it like? "Obscene. But that was the point. It's a big square cut stone, aquamarine. You can't type with it on because it's so heavy. It's one of those things you have to bring out on certain occasions; it's not day-to-day because you could really hurt someone with it."

She also saw the third installment in her series published. On Thursday, July 8, 1999, Bloomsbury released *Harry Potter and the Prisoner of Azkaban*. Bookstores were instructed not to start selling copies until 3:45 P.M., the time when British schools let out. Tara Stephenson, the head of sales at Blackwell's Children's Bookshop in Oxford, said that once the witching hour had arrived, "There was a pause, then once the first one was sold, it was an absolute tidal wave."[127] By 4:15 P.M., Blackwell's had sold ninety-two copies of the new book.

The scene was repeated throughout the United Kingdom. A bookshop in Birmingham sold thirty-two copies in the first ten minutes. A book store in the small town of Thirsk sold fifty-six in the first afternoon. Within two weeks, the book had gone through ten printings and had sold in excess of 270,000 copies, knocking Thomas Harris's novel about fictional serial killer Hannibal Lector off the top of British best-seller lists. "I haven't seen anything like this," said Caroline Horn, an editor with *Bookseller* magazine. "It happened in the playground."[128]

Once again, impatient readers in the United States began ordering the book online, much to the chagrin of executives at Scholastic Publishing. Arthur Levine was not happy to see potential U.S. sales vanishing again, yet he did not want to appear angry with Harry Potter fans for being eager to read the next installment of the series. The American publisher was determined to not let the Internet spoil the debut of Rowling's next book, however. Scholastic and Bloomsbury agreed to release Rowling's as-yet-unnamed fourth book simultaneously in Britain and America.

A Need for Privacy

Amid all her success, Rowling struggled to keep her life as normal as possible at home on Hazelbank Terrace. Jessica had started primary school after turning five in 1998, and Rowling routinely walked her daughter to school in the morning and met her at the school gate in the afternoon. Rowling also continued to do all of her own shopping. One day, a literary agent named Giles Gordon recognized Rowling as she waited in line ahead of him in a delicatessen. "I remember being struck by the totally easy way she was talking to her daughter," he later said. "It was very affectionate and down-to-earth. They were totally relaxed together and I thought there was a very good bond between them which I thought was awfully nice."[129]

When Gordon wrote about the encounter in his gossip column in the *Edinburgh Evening News,* however, Rowling stopped shopping at that store. "Thanks a lot," said a person who worked behind the counter the next time he saw Gordon. "Ever since you wrote the piece, we haven't seen her. She was one of our best customers."[130]

Rowling has remained fiercely protective of Jessica's privacy. When the British magazine *OK* published photographs of her and Jessica on a private hotel beach in Mauritius, an island in the Indian Ocean, in 2001, Rowling filed a complaint with the Press Complaints Commission (PCC). Rowling maintained that the publication of the photographs, the first ever published of Jessica, violated a rule in the newspaper code of practice that forbids the publication of pictures of children just because their parents are famous. In October 2001, the PCC upheld the complaint.

Despite such events, Rowling believes that Jessica has remained unfazed by her mother's celebrity status. "I think in one sense the blessing is that she was too young when it started to really notice a difference," Rowling explained. "She's kind of grown up with this as the norm." Nor does Jessica seem threatened by the "other" child in the house, the apprentice wizard who occupies so much of her mother's time. "She knows, and she's right, that she's top dog,"[131] Rowling said.

In fact, Jessica seems to be as big of a Harry Potter fan as anyone else. Rowling has revealed that she started reading the series to her daughter sooner than she had planned to. "Initially I said I wouldn't start reading them to her until she was seven, because I do think some of the themes are a little demanding for five-year-olds," Rowling said. "But I cracked and started reading them to her at six, because she was at school and she was surrounded by kids asking her about Harry Potter. I thought it was mean, because she wasn't part of this enormous part of my life and I felt I was excluding her, so I read them to her."[132]

Finding Time for Fans

As Rowling's success continued to build, she began to attend book signings, where she met many fans. The new author found these encounters to be the most enjoyable aspect of her sudden fame. "My favorite was the girl who came to the Edinburgh Book Festival to see me," she recalled. "When she reached the signing table she said, 'I didn't want so many people to be here—this is MY book.' That really resonated with me, because that's how I feel about my own favorite books."[133]

Rowling has been amazed by some children's reactions to her work. "I met a boy at a school in England who recited the first page of the first book to me from memory," the author recalled. "When he stopped, he said, 'I can go on.' He continued reciting the first five pages of the book. That was unbelievable."[134]

Although she had appeared at many book signings in Great Britain, Rowling said that she did not fully appreciate the im-

Rowling signs a book for an admirer outfitted in a wizard's cape.

pact her work was having on children until she toured the United States in 1999. "I don't think I really realized how many [fans] there were until I visited the States in October, and met thousands and thousands of people at book signings," Rowling recalled. "For the first time I realized how many children love Harry. It was a moving experience for me."[135]

"Huge Gaping Hole"

After returning to the United Kingdom from her U.S. tour, Rowling settled in to complete the next installment of her seven-book series. It would turn out to be the most difficult of the books to write. For one thing, it was much longer than the first three books. "I knew from the beginning it would be the biggest of the first four," Rowling later said. "It's a complex plot, and you don't rush a plot that complex, because everyone's gonna get confused."[136]

As it turned out, even the author herself got confused. Halfway through the book, Rowling discovered a problem with the plot. "I should have put that plot under a microscope," Rowling later told *Entertainment Weekly*. "I wrote what I thought was half the book, and 'Ack!' Huge gaping hole in the middle of the plot." Rowling had created one character, a cousin of the Weasley boys, who served roughly the same function as Rita Skeeter, the investigative journalist who also appeared in the story. Rowling realized that one of the characters had to go. Since Skeeter would be important to later books, Rowling decided to pull out the Weasley cousin, creating what she later referred to jokingly as "the phantom character of 'Harry Potter.'"[137] Because Rowling's plots and subplots are tightly entwined, she found that she had to unbraid and reweave nearly half of the book. Rowling wrote for ten hours a day to get the book back on schedule. Despite the effort, she missed her deadline by two months.

"Harry Potter IV"

When she finally completed the book, Rowling agreed to meet with the press to promote her latest work. Throughout the interviews, Rowling refused to divulge the title of the book. Critics said the silence was a strategy designed to build interest in it. Rowling disputed the charge. "It wasn't even a marketing ploy," she said. "It came from me. This book was the culmination of ten years' work, and something very big in terms of my ongoing plot happens at the end," she explained. "Had that got out, there's no way the book would have been as enjoyable to read."[138]

To preserve the secret, no advance copies were given to reviewers or members of the press. The printers shipped the books in boxes marked "HARRY POTTER IV, NOT TO BE SOLD BEFORE JULY 8, 2000."[139] Worried that someone might raid the Bloomsbury offices to get a peek at the book, Rowling's editor Emma Mathewson locked the original manuscript in a bank vault. Despite the precautions, the cover jacket and the title, *Harry Potter and the Goblet of Fire,* leaked out on June 26. A few days later, a clerk at a Wal-Mart in Virginia who did not know about Scholastic's retailing plans sold a copy of the book to eight-year-old Laura Cantwell of Fairfax, who shared her lucky find with the media.

Despite all efforts to keep the title of Rowling's fourth book a secret, it was leaked two weeks before the June 26, 2000, selling date.

The leaks did nothing to spoil the book's debut. Thousands of children lined up at bookstores in Britain, Canada, and the United States to buy the first copies. Some bookstores stayed open past midnight on July 7 so that fans could buy the book at 12:01 A.M. Enterprising booksellers such as Steve Moore of Toronto dressed up as wizards and hosted pajama parties to celebrate the midnight event. The Tattered Cover Bookstore in Denver, Colorado, served late-night patrons a brew of ginger ale and apple juice to mimic Harry Potter's favorite beverage, butter beer. One thousand people showed up at Vancouver's Kidsbooks for a publication party at 11:00 P.M., but co-owners Phyllis Simon and Kelly McKinnon had to turn half of the crowd away. "Five hundred is all the fire regulations would allow,"[140] explained Simon.

To promote the book, Bloomsbury arranged for Rowling to take a four-day trip around Britain in a vintage train decorated as the Hogwarts Express. A special Platform 9¾ was rigged up at King's Cross station, where Rowling was to board the train on July 8. The train was scheduled to depart at 11:00 A.M.—the time the Hogwarts Express leaves to take the young wizards to

Fans wave at the departing Hogwarts Express. The size of the crowd prompted police to rush Rowling onto the train before she could greet her fans.

school at the beginning of the term. Rowling arrived at the station in a turquoise Ford Anglia and found more than five hundred excited fans waiting to see her. To maintain control, police officers hustled Rowling past the crowd and onto the train without her having the chance to say as much as a hello. Embarrassed, the author opened the window as the train pulled away and called out an apology to her disappointed fans.

It was the only disappointment of the day. Online retailer Amazon.com teamed up with Federal Express to deliver 250,000 copies of the book on the first day at no extra charge to their customers. Amazon reported that it had logged 325,000 preorders in the weeks leading up to the publication—eight times more than its previous high. Scholastic ordered the largest first printing in history, 3.8 million copies for the United States alone. Bloomsbury also ordered the largest print run in its history. Rowling stood to earn $10 million in royalties when the first printings sold out, which they shortly did.

From Success to Celebrity

The next week Harry landed on the covers of *Newsweek* in the United States and *Maclean's* in Canada. *Newsweek* reviewer Malcolm Jones raved, "The highest compliment I can pay 'Harry Potter and the Goblet of Fire' is to say that from beginning to end, it made me want to stay up all night—or as long as it took to finish it. Rowling has gotten better with every book, and this time things move so smoothly that the story doesn't seem written so much as it seems to unfold on its own."[141]

In October, Rowling visited Canada to attend a fund-raising lunch for children's literature, meet her fans, and give a public reading of her work. Much to her amazement, she was treated like a rock star. Fifteen thousand fans—mostly children—crowded into Toronto's SkyDome baseball stadium to see her. Greeted by a thunderous ovation, Rowling said, "I'm delighted—and terrified—to be here." Her fourteen-minute reading delighted her fans. "It'll be a memory for the rest of my life, like a historical date,"[142] said nine-year-old Iain McCann.

When Rowling returned home from Canada, she discovered that the *Sunday Times* ranked her as the 526th wealthiest person and the 36th wealthiest woman in the United Kingdom. Thanks to the record-breaking success of *Harry Potter and the Goblet of Fire,* Rowling's novels had sold a total of 76 million copies, boosting her wealth to an estimated £65 million ($97.5 million). *Time* magazine named Rowling as one of its runners-up for Person of the Year, praising her for having "turned on a new generation to that old technology, the wondrous printed word."[143]

Time also noted Rowling's contributions to charity. She donated $725,000 to the National Council for One Parent Families and agreed to be the charity's first spokesperson. She also announced that she would publish two books for the benefit of Comic Relief U.K., a charity that helps children in developing nations.

Novel Fund-Raisers

The two fund-raising books, *Quidditch Through the Ages* and *Fantastic Beasts and Where to Find Them,* do not tell stories. Instead, they catalog information about the magical world in which

Natalie McDonald

J.K. Rowling receives thousands of letters from adoring fans, but one
letter touched her more deeply than any other. In an article titled
"The Rowling Connection," Brian Bethune of *Maclean's* magazine told
the story in the November 6, 2000, issue.

> In Toronto, nine-year-old Natalie McDonald was dying. "She was
> obsessed with the Harry Potter books," remembers family friend
> and political activist Annie Kidder. "They had been her respite
> from the hell of leukemia. And because I'm the sort of person
> who thinks there must be *something* I can do, I badgered Rowl-
> ing's publishers in London, sending them a letter and an e-mail
> and a fax for her."
>
> Passed on by the publishers, the letter arrived at Rowling's Edin-
> burgh home a day after the author had left for a holiday in
> Spain. "When I came back two weeks later and read it, I had a
> bad feeling I was too late," Rowling told *Maclean's*. "I tried to
> phone Annie but she wasn't in, so I e-mailed both Natalie and
> her mother, Valerie—because Annie hadn't told Valerie what
> she had done." Rowling was right in her foreboding—the e-mails
> were received the day after Natalie died on Aug. 3.
>
> "Jo's e-mail was beautiful," Kidder says. "She didn't patronize Na-
> talie, or tell her everything was OK; she addressed her as a human
> being who was going through a hard time. She talked about her
> books and her characters and which ones she liked best."
>
> The story might have ended there, but Valerie McDonald wrote
> back, in thanks. "That letter touched deep," Rowling says
> slowly, trying to explain the esteem in which she holds Natalie's
> mother. . . . So a regular correspondence began, and an unex-
> pected friendship. . . . But even before that, the author had
> quietly commemorated the reader she never met. On page 159
> of *Goblet of Fire,* the famous sorting hat of Hogwarts School of
> Witchcraft and Wizardry sends first-year student Natalie Mc-
> Donald—the only real person in any of Rowling's novels—to
> Harry's own Gryffindor house.

Harry Potter and the other wizards live. Both titles appear in the
fictional library of Hogwarts School. According to Rowling's
novels, *Quidditch Through the Ages* was written by Kennilworthy
Whisp and *Fantastic Beasts and Where to Find Them* was the work
of Newt Scamander; these are the names that appear on the title
pages of the fund-raising books. The companies that normally
would receive a profit from the sale of Rowling's books agreed

to donate their proceeds to Comic Relief U.K. As a result, more than 80 percent of the money raised by the sale of these books went to aid programs in the United Kingdom, the poorer areas of Africa, and elsewhere around the world.

Christopher Little announced that Rowling's two books for charity would be her only new works to appear in 2001. Her fifth book, *Harry Potter and the Order of the Phoenix,* would not be available until 2002. The announcement led to speculation in the press that Rowling was experiencing writer's block, the inability to write anything new. Noting "several columns of total fabrication" on the topic in a local newspaper, Rowling decided to respond. "I made it clear last summer that I wanted to take the time to make sure that book five was not dashed off to meet a deadline," she wrote to the newspaper, "but was completed to my full satisfaction as its predecessors have been, as I was committed to producing two additional books for Comic Relief this year."[144]

At the age of thirty-five, J.K. Rowling had accomplished more than she had ever thought possible. She had published not one but four best-selling books. She was able to use her talents and notoriety to help promote social causes, just as her hero Jessica Mitford had. She had accumulated wealth far beyond her wildest dreams. As 2001 dawned, Rowling was about to see another of her dreams come true. A longtime fan of the movies, she was about to see the characters from her own imagination take on new life on the big screen.

Chapter 7

Lights, Camera, Quidditch!

As soon as *Harry Potter and the Philosopher's Stone* was published, film executives began to envision the story of the apprentice wizard as a motion picture. Less than a month after the book was released, four film companies—two British, two American—had made Rowling offers for the rights to her novel. Neither Rowling nor Christopher Little was in a rush to proceed, however. They wanted to establish a successful book series first. That way they would be in a position to exert some control over what kind of film would be made. Their strategy paid off. After the success of the first three books, Rowling and Little were able to make a motion picture deal that met all of their financial and artistic requirements. The end result would be a movie that not only pleased the author but also set box-office records.

Rowling insisted from the start that any movie made from her books would have to be live action, not animated. No new characters would be introduced and none could be eliminated. "What was most important to me was . . . that they did not take my characters and take them off to do something that I didn't want them to do . . . because I am obviously in the middle of a seven-book series,"[145] Rowling later said. The U.S. motion picture company Warner Bros. agreed to these terms, and in late 1999, Rowling signed a deal with the studio for about $1 million.

The Right Director

The first thing the studio had to do was find the right person to direct the movie. Steven Spielberg showed interest in directing the project, but later decided to pass on it. "I have every certainty that the series of 'Harry Potter' movies will be phenomenally successful," Spielberg said in a prepared statement. "J.K. Rowling's vision of Harry Potter is modern genius. Warner Bros. and [President] Alan Horn have been more than generous in the time they've allowed me to make a decision. However, at this time, my directorial interests are taking me in another direction."[146]

After interviewing several possible candidates, Warner Bros. gave the directing job to Chris Columbus, the director of box-office hits *Home Alone* and *Mrs. Doubtfire*. Columbus had also been a screenwriter on live-action fantasy films such as *Gremlins,*

Whose Stone?

J.K. Rowling called her first book *Harry Potter and the Philosopher's Stone*. The title refers to the legendary stone thought to be capable of turning base metals such as lead into gold and restoring youth to the aged. The executives at Scholastic who purchased the American rights to the book, however, had doubts about the title. "It was felt that 'Philosopher' was not a word familiar to young Americans," reported Sean Smith in his book *J.K. Rowling: A Biography*. Focusing on the stone's magical properties, the Scholastic executives suggested that "Sorcerer" replace "Philosopher" in the title.

Rowling, who tends to respect young readers more than many adults do, opposed the effort to rename her book. Not being an expert on American culture, however, she at last deferred to her publisher's judgment. The book appeared in the United States as *Harry Potter and the Sorcerer's Stone,* and throughout the novel the characters refer to the magic stone by its newfangled name.

The dual titles presented a problem when Warner Bros. began to make a motion picture based on the book. Afraid of alienating fans who had come to know the book by a certain title, Warner Bros. decided to continue the name game: The movie would be released in the United Kingdom as *Harry Potter and the Philosopher's Stone* and in the United States as *Harry Potter and the Sorcerer's Stone*. Scenes in which the characters mention the artifact had to be filmed twice to reflect the Old and New World differences.

Is the difference important? For those who simply enjoy an exciting story, probably not, but for those whose reading experience is deepened and enriched by Rowling's artful brew of historical, mythological, and literary references, the absence of the Philosopher's Stone from the American edition may take a bit of the luster off of the book.

The Goonies, and *Young Sherlock Holmes.* "It was important to us to find a director who has an affinity for both children and magic,"[147] said Lorenzo di Bonaventura, Warner Bros. president of worldwide theatrical production.

The task of adapting the book to a screenplay was given to Steve Kloves, a Hollywood veteran who had written sceenplays for the critically acclaimed coming-of-age movie *Racing with the Moon* (1984), the love story *The Fabulous Baker Boys* (1988), and the comedy *Wonder Boys* (2000). "I've never been involved with a picture that anyone was remotely interested in before I'd handed in the script,"[148] Kloves told the online magazine *Salon.com.* However, Kloves saw difficulties with bringing Rowling's book to the screen:

> Adapting the first book in the series is tough because the plot doesn't lend itself to adaptation as well as the next two books; Volumes 2 and 3 lay out more naturally as movies, since the plots are more compact and have more narrative drive. The first one is about exposing you to this world of a boy who grows up in a cabinet and finds out who he really is—that he is the son of wizards who are now dead and that he has inherited their talent— and then goes to a school to explore that talent.[149]

For the movie to be successful, Kloves decided he had to focus on the characters more than the plot. "Obviously you need a plot, but the charm of the movie should be these kids, and you have to be as faithful as possible," he said. "The picture has to be British, and it has to be true to the kids."[150]

The Search

Next, the movie had to be cast. A fan of the movies, Rowling had given some thought to who might play some of her characters. She suggested that Robbie Coltrane, the burly Scottish actor who played Falstaff in the 1989 film of Shakespeare's *Henry V,* would be perfect for the part of Hagrid, the giant Hogwarts groundskeeper. Columbus agreed, and Coltrane accepted the role. Irish film star Richard Harris, who had played King Arthur in the 1967 musical *Camelot,* signed on to play Dumbledore.

Two-time Academy Award–winning actress Dame Maggie Smith was cast as Professor McGonagall. Monty Python veteran John Cleese played Nearly Headless Nick, a ghost that haunts the Hogwarts dining hall.

A search began to find the children who would play Harry Potter, Hermione Granger, and Ron Weasley. Ten-year-old Emma Watson won the part of Harry's gal pal, and eleven-year-old Rupert Grint was cast as Ron. The search continued for a suitable Harry. Before it was over, sixty thousand boys had auditioned for the role. Even Rowling joined the hunt for her hero. "I am now walking around in London and Edinburgh, and I'm looking at kids as I pass them, just thinking, Could be, you never know," Rowling told *Newsweek* in July 2000. "I may just lunge at this kid and say, 'Can you act? You're coming with me. Taxi!'"[151]

It was not Rowling but Warner Bros. executive David Heyman who found the perfect boy to play Harry. Heyman attended a London play with his friend Alan Radcliffe, who brought along his eleven-year-old son, Daniel. "I was watching the play but the details melted into the background after I saw Dan," Heyman recalled. "I thought Dan so clearly embodied the spirit of Harry."[152]

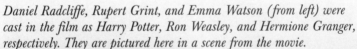

Daniel Radcliffe, Rupert Grint, and Emma Watson (from left) were cast in the film as Harry Potter, Ron Weasley, and Hermione Granger, respectively. They are pictured here in a scene from the movie.

Director Chris Columbus agreed. "There were times when we felt we would never find an individual who embodied the complex spirit and depth of Harry Potter," said Columbus. "Then, Dan walked into the room and we all knew we had found Harry." Rowling, too, was satisfied with the selection. "Having seen Dan Radcliffe's screen test, I don't think Chris Columbus could have found a better Harry," she said. "I wish Dan, Emma and Rupert the very best of luck and hope they have as much fun acting the first year at Hogwarts as I had writing it." [153]

Cashing In on the Craze

As work on the film progressed, various companies looked for ways to capitalize on the movie's almost certain success. The Warner Bros. Consumer Products division began to license the Harry Potter name to certain companies. Soft drink giant Coca Cola paid £100 million ($150 million) to sponsor the film, which cost £85 million ($125 million) to make. Johnson & Johnson bought the rights to market a Harry Potter shampoo that featured a cut-out lightning bolt in the center of the bottle. Elec-

Daniel Radcliffe and Harry Potter *director Chris Columbus enjoy a laugh.*

tronic Arts gained the rights to manufacture electronic games based on the stories, and toy giant Mattel was granted permission to make action figures of Harry Potter, Hermione, Ron Weasley, Draco Malfoy, Hagrid, the mountain troll, and Professors Snape and Quirrell. Amid all of the dealmaking, Rowling retained her trademark sense of humor. "If the action figures are horrible, tell the kids I said don't buy them,"[154] she said.

The filming of *Harry Potter and the Philosopher's Stone* ended in April, and the first trailer, or preview, was released in June. Harry Potter fans were delighted by their first glimpses of the movie, including the expert computer animation. By the time the movie premiered on November 2, 2001, more than £1 million ($1.5 million) worth of tickets had been presold.

World Premiere

The premiere was held at the Odeon theater in Leicester Square, London. Set designers decorated the front of the theater to look like Hogwarts School. About five thousand fans—many dressed up in wizard hats and cloaks—showed up to get a glimpse of Rowling and other celebrities. Specially invited guests had access to temporary bleachers set up near the theater entrance, but everyone else had to stand behind metal barriers that lined the walkway leading up to the theater. Large video screens set up around the square gave those in the crowd a televised view of the celebrities. Right before the celebrities began to arrive, some of the children who were waiting behind the barricades were picked out of the crowd and given seats in the bleachers.

Rowling attended the premiere with Dr. Neil Murray, an anesthetist whom Rowling had met at a party given by a mutual friend the year before. Taking in the hysteria that greeted her arrival, Rowling remarked, "This is not what you think about when you write a book." Daniel Radcliffe, the star of the movie, agreed, calling the experience "overwhelming but fantastic." "It is so cool," he said. "I have never heard my name shouted so much in an hour."[155]

Costars Rupert Grint and Emma Watson also attended the event, as did director Chris Columbus. Many celebrities also turned up, including actor Ben Stiller, Australian actress Cate

A thrilled Rowling attends the London premiere of Harry Potter *with her future husband, Dr. Neil Murray.*

Blanchett, pop star Sting, Duchess of York Sarah Ferguson, and her two daughters Princesses Beatrice and Eugenie. Afterward, Ferguson said, "It is brilliant. I thoroughly enjoyed it and the girls loved it." Rowling said she was "happy and relieved" by how faithful the film is to her creation. "It went wonderfully. I am so pleased, everyone seems to love it."[156]

Not quite everyone was enchanted with the production. Elvis Mitchell of the *New York Times* complained that the movie followed the book too closely for its own good:

> The world may not be ready yet for the film equivalent of books on tape, but this peculiar phenomenon has arrived in the form of the film adaptation of J.K. Rowling's "Harry Potter and the Sorcerer's Stone." The most highly awaited movie of the year has a dreary, literal-minded competence, following the letter of the law as laid down by the author. A lack of imagination pervades the movie because it so slavishly follows the book. The

filmmakers, the producers and the studio seem panicked by anything that might feel like a departure from the book—which already feels film-ready—so "Harry Potter and the Sorcerer's Stone" never takes on a life of its own. Someone has cast a sleepwalker's spell over the proceedings, and at nearly two and a half hours you may go under, too.[157]

The *Los Angeles Times* agreed. "The result is a remarkably faithful copy of the book that treats the text like holy writ," wrote film critic Kenneth Turan. "Ideally, as in something like 'The English Patient' or 'The Godfather,' a film will extend or even transcend the book's emotional territory and bring a touch of cinematic poetry to the proceedings. But to get that, you have to take risks, and risk is something no one associated with this project wanted anything to do with."[158]

Most children did not share the critics' view. "The movie skipped part of the book, but I thought it was great," said ten-year-old Jeffrey Chyau of New York. "I thought it was really good, the special effects were good, but it was too long," said fifteen-year-old Marisa Bass of the Bronx. However, Bass also felt that the movie robbed her of her own private experience with the book. "Now, Book 1 is done for me," she said. "The vision is glazed in your mind now that Hollywood has claimed it. If I were to read Book 1 again, I would think of it like the movie, which is why I was hesitant to see it."[159]

Box-Office Magic

Since Rowling's books had garnered a worldwide legion of fans numbering in the tens of millions, studio executives expected a large turnout for the movie, but few expected the film to set records. Nevertheless, *Harry Potter and the Sorcerer's Stone* broke the single-day record for movie receipts in the United States, raking in $31.6 million the first day. The previous single-day record had been held by *Star Wars Episode 1: The Phantom Menace*, which earned $28.5 million on its opening day in 1999. The boy wizard's new record stood for only a day, however, as the film earned $32.9 million on Saturday. Paul Dergarabedian, president of Exhibitor Relations Company in Los Angeles, was amazed. "These grosses are unprecedented," he said, "no film has ever done over $30 million in a single day, and here it's done it twice!"[160]

On Sunday, the movie earned another $29 million, pushing receipts for the opening weekend to $93.5 million—yet another

A Harry Potter Book Burning

As the motion picture version of *Harry Potter and the Sorcerer's Stone* swept to new heights of popularity, some Americans became convinced that the Harry Potter craze was poisoning the minds of impressionable children. With scenes of broomstick riding, incantations, and the summoning of spirits, Rowling's books struck some conservative Christians as a glamorization of witchcraft and Satanism. CNN.com reported that Jack Brock, the founder and pastor of Christ Community Church in Alamogordo, New Mexico, called the Harry Potter series "a masterpiece of satanic deception."

On December 30, 2001, Brock led his congregation in the ceremonial burning of Rowling's books. "These books teach children how they can get into witchcraft and become a witch, wizard or warlock," Brock declared. The Associated Press reported that members of Brock's congregation sang "Amazing Grace" as they threw copies of the Harry Potter books into the fire.

The anti-Potter protests were not limited to New Mexico, however. Parents in California, Michigan, Minnesota, New York, and South Carolina have called for the removal of Rowling's books from classrooms and school libraries because of fears that they promote an interest in the occult.

J.K. Rowling is mystified by the movement to ban her books, and in an interview with Shelagh Rogers on the Canadian Broadcasting Corporation's "This Morning Sunday Edition," she dismissed the idea that her works promote the dark arts. "First of all, I would question whether these people have actually read the books. I really would question that," Rowling said. "These books are absolutely not about devil worship. I vacillate between feeling faintly annoyed that I'm being so misrepresented, and finding the whole thing really quite funny. Because it is laughable that someone would say that of these books."

Author Judy Blume, whose own books have been under attack for years, thinks Rowling is taking the challenges to her work too lightly. In an editorial that appeared in the *New York Times* on October 22, 1999, Blume wrote, "The real danger is not in the books, but in laughing off those who would ban them. The protests against Harry Potter follow a tradition that has been growing since the early 1980's and often leaves school principals trembling with fear that is then passed down to teachers and librarians."

record. The previous three-day high record was $72.1 million, set in 1997 by *The Lost World: Jurassic Park*. Dan Fellman, head of distribution for Warner Bros. could not have been more pleased. "I'm so excited with the performance of this movie in America, we have shattered every existing industry record," he said. "We just feel absolutely sensational!"[161]

Box-office records were set in the United Kingdom as well. *Harry Potter and the Philosopher's Stone* took in £16 million on its first day, nearly doubling the previous record of *Star Wars Episode 1: The Phantom Menace*, which took in £9.5 million in 1999.

Harry Potter and the Sorcerer's Stone ended the year as the number one film in the United States, earning an estimated $286.1 million in less than two months.

Happily Ever After

With her fortunes soaring, Rowling decided to buy a home in London so she could be closer to her publisher and the center of British culture. She purchased a mansion in a posh area of London for £4.5 million ($6.75 million). The Georgian-style residence has an underground swimming pool and twenty-four-hour security. In November, Rowling also purchased a country retreat known as Killiechassie House, located on the banks of the Tay near Aberfeldy in Scotland. Built in 1865, the seven-bedroom estate sits on twelve acres of land.

It was on this estate that Rowling capped off her momentous year by marrying Dr. Neil Murray in a private ceremony on Boxing Day, December 26. Among the fifteen guests were Rowling's father, Peter, and her stepmother, Barbara. Jessica, who was then eight years old, was one of Rowling's three bridesmaids. Dr. Murray's parents, Ernest and Barbara Murray, of Huntley, Aberdeenshire, also attended the twenty-minute ceremony. The couple reportedly did not have time to take a honeymoon.

Murray, who is six years younger than Rowling, resigned from his £32,000-a-year post as a senior house officer at St. John's Hospital in Livingstone shortly after meeting Rowling, presumably so he could accompany her on her worldwide book tours. Sources close to the couple dismissed the idea that Murray

has retired permanently, insisting that Murray was determined
to maintain his independence and had plans to become a family
practitioner.

More to Do

Rowling was not about to retire, either. After completing *Harry
Potter and the Order of the Phoenix,* she will have two more install-
ments of her series to write. "The books are all planned and I
desperately do want to write to the end of the story," she told a
reporter. "I see it as one huge novel." [162] In addition, Warner
Bros. has expressed a desire to make all seven books into motion pictures, with the release of *Harry Potter and the Chamber of
Secrets* slated for November 15, 2002. If Rowling continues to be
involved with the movies, she could spend much of the next several years consulting on the movies and promoting them.

In addition, Rowling plans to continue her charity work, acting as a spokesperson for the National Council of One Parent
Families and making contributions to Comic Relief U.K. Rowling is also very involved in the battle against multiple sclerosis
(MS), the disease that claimed her mother's life. Rowling donated
£250,000 ($375,000) to the MS Society in Scotland to open a re-
source center for sufferers of the disease in Aberdeen. "I look
forward to the day when this kind of center is the norm rather
than the exception," she said. "The truth about the appalling
poor quality of care available to people with MS only became
clear to me after I had been in touch with the MS Society in Scotland, which makes me doubly proud to be its patron." [163]

Although Rowling finds the movie business and her charity
work to be interesting, they remain sidelights to her true pas-
sion: writing. Whatever else she does with her life, Rowling will
always continue to write. What she will write after the Harry
Potter series remains a mystery, even to her. She told BBC
Radio Gloucestershire's Nigel Ballard that she will probably try
her hand at something completely different. "Maybe I'll write
something about an obscure medieval monk," [164] she said.

Some observers doubt that Rowling will ever be able to
write anything that approaches the quality and popularity of the
Harry Potter series. Although she may never again be struck

Order of the British Empire

In June 2000, a spokesperson for Queen Elizabeth II of Great Britain announced that the queen would award J.K. Rowling the Order of the British Empire, one of the nation's highest honors, for her "services to children's literature."

Rowling was supposed to receive the insignia during a ceremony at Buckingham Palace in December, but she canceled her appearance on account of illness. Instead, she received the award on March 2, 2001, from Charles, the Prince of Wales. According to an account of the ceremony that appeared in the *London Times,* Prince Charles, who also is the author of a children's book, revealed that he was a fan of Harry Potter by asking Rowling if the upcoming movie was "as good as

the book." Rowling assured the prince that it was. "The Prince asked me about the film," Rowling told reporters after the ceremony. "He said he can't wait, and he wanted to know whether it was true how I saw the story in my mind. I said that it was."

Rowling said she was "delighted and honored" to receive the award.

Rowling proudly displays the Order of the British Empire insignia.

with a lightning bolt of inspiration like the one she experienced on the train between Manchester and London, by the time she finishes the series she will have at least a decade of experience as a novelist to draw on for her next work, whatever it might be.

Rowling says that she has already written the last chapter of the final book in the Harry Potter series and that "the last word is 'scar.'" [165] If Rowling never writes another word after that, she will have already achieved immortality as the creator of the orphan boy who learned he was a wizard just in time to take up his wand against the dark forces threatening the world.

Notes

Introduction: "I'm Not Going to Be Famous"

1. Quoted in Roxanne Feldman, "The Truth About Harry," *School Library Journal,* September 1, 1999. http://slj.reviewsnews.com/index.asp?layout=articleArchive&articleId=CA153024&display=searchResults&stt=001.
2. Paul Gray, "The Magic of Potter," *Time,* December 25, 2000– January 1, 2001, p. 116.
3. Quoted in Gray, "The Magic of Potter," p. 118.
4. Quoted in Gray, "The Magic of Potter," p. 118.
5. Quoted in Rose Cox, "Harry Potter Books Inspire New Love for Literature," *Anchorage Daily News,* January 26, 2002.

Chapter 1: Young Storyteller

6. Quoted in Elizabeth Gleick, "The Wizard of Hogwarts," *Time,* April 12, 1999, p. 86.
7. Quoted in Sean Smith, *J.K. Rowling: A Biography.* London: Michael O'Mara Books, 2001, p. 20.
8. Quoted in Lindsey Fraser, *Conversations with J.K. Rowling.* New York: Scholastic, 2000, p. 11.
9. Quoted in Helena de Bertodano, "Harry Potter Charms a Nation," *Daily Telegraph,* July 25, 1998. www.telegraph.co.uk/et?ac=00193 7575942258&pg=/et/98/7/25/borow25.html.
10. J.K. Rowling, *The Not Especially Fascinating Life So Far of JK Rowling.* www.cliphoto.com/potter/rowling.htm.
11. Rowling, *The Not Especially Fascinating Life So Far of JK Rowling.*
12. Quoted in Helen M. Jerome and Jerome V. Kramer, "Author's Childhood Friend Says He Was Inspiration for Harry Potter," *Book,* March/April 2000. www.bookmagazine.com/archive/issue9/potter.shtml.

13. Interview with J.K. Rowling, *This Morning Sunday Edition*, Canadian Broadcasting Corporation, October 23, 2000. http://radio. cbc.ca/programs/thismorning/sites/books/rowling_001023.html.

14. Rowling, *The Not Especially Fascinating Life So Far of JK Rowling*.

15. Rowling, *The Not Especially Fascinating Life So Far of JK Rowling*.

16. Interview with J.K. Rowling, *Amazon.co.uk*. www.cliphoto.com/ potter/interview.htm.

17. Chat transcript with J.K. Rowling, *Barnesandnoble.com*, HP Galleries, March 19, 1999. http://history.250x.com/vaults/c105.htm.

18. Quoted in Bertodano, "Harry Potter Charms a Nation."

19. Quoted in Feldman, "The Truth About Harry."

20. Quoted in "J.K. Rowling Frequently Asked Questions." www.harry potterfans.net/jkr/bio.html.

21. Rowling, *The Not Especially Fascinating Life So Far of JK Rowling*.

22. Quoted in Simon Hattenstone, "Harry, Jessie and Me," *Guardian Unlimited*, July 8, 2000. http://books.guardian.co.uk/departments/ childrenandteens/story/0,6000,340844,00.html.

23. Quoted in Elisabeth Dunn, "From Dole to Hollywood," *Daily Telegraph*, August 2, 1997. www.telegraph.co.uk/et?ac= 00193757 5942258&pg=/et/97/8/2/bodole02.html.

24. J.K. Rowling, *Harry Potter and the Chamber of Secrets*. New York: Scholastic, 1999, p. v.

25. Rowling, *The Not Especially Fascinating Life So Far of JK Rowling*.

26. Quoted in Malcolm Jones, "The Return of Harry Potter!" *Newsweek*, July 10, 2000, p. 60.

Chapter 2: The Growth of an Idea

27. Quoted in Fraser, *Conversations with J.K. Rowling*, p. 38.

28. Quoted in Jones, "The Return of Harry Potter!" p. 60.

29. Quoted in Malcolm Jones, "Magician for Millions," *Newsweek*, August 23, 1999, p. 59.

30. Quoted in Jones, "The Return of Harry Potter!" p. 60.

31. Quoted in Jones, "The Return of Harry Potter!" p. 58.

32. Quoted in Fraser, *Conversations with J.K. Rowling*, p. 38.

33. Online interview with J.K. Rowling, *Scholastic.com*, February 3, 2000. www. scholastic.com/harrypotter/author/transcript1.htm.

34. Quoted in "Questions and Answers with J.K. Rowling." www. teachervision.com/lesson-plans/lesson-2693.html.

35. Quoted in Fraser, *Conversations with J.K. Rowling*, pp. 26–27.

36. Quoted in Fraser, *Conversations with J.K. Rowling*, p. 39.

37. Chat transcript with Rowling, *Barnesandnoble.com*.

38. Marina Warner, "Fantasy's Power and Peril," *New York Times Online,* December 16, 2001. www.nytimes.com/2001/12/16/weekin review/16WARN.html.

39. Maurine Dowd, "Veni, Vidi, Voldemort," *New York Times,* December 9, 2001, section 4, p. 13.

40. Quoted in Fraser, *Conversations with J.K. Rowling,* p. 31.

41. Quoted in Fraser, *Conversations with J.K. Rowling,* pp. 40–41.

42. Quoted in Fraser, *Conversations with J.K. Rowling,* p. 20.

43. Quoted in Fraser, *Conversations with J.K. Rowling,* p. 17.

44. Quoted in Margaret Weir, "Of Magic and Single Motherhood," *Salon.com,* March 31, 1999. www.salon.com/mwt/feature/1999/ 03/cov_31featureb.html.

45. Chat transcript with Rowling, *Barnesandnoble.com.*

46. Quoted in Linda Richards, "January Profile: J.K. Rowling," *January Magazine.* www.januarymagazine.com/profiles/jkrowling.html.

47. Interview with Rowling, *Amazon.co.uk.* www.cliphoto.com/potter/ interview.htm.

48. Quoted in Nancy Gibbs, "Harry Is an Old Soul," *Time,* December 25, 2000–January 1, 2001, p. 119.

49. Online interview with Rowling, *Scholastic.com,* October 16, 2000. www. scholastic.com/harrypotter/author/transcript2.htm.

50. Chat transcript with Rowling, *Barnesandnoble.com.*

51. Quoted in Jones, "Magician for Millions," p. 59.

52. Interview with Rowling, *This Morning Sunday Edition.*

53. Interview with Rowling, *This Morning Sunday Edition.*

54. Interview with Rowling, *This Morning Sunday Edition.*

55. Quoted in "Meet J.K. Rowling." www. scholastic.com/harrypotter/ author/index.htm.

Chapter 3: Loss and Love

56. Quoted in Matt Seaton, "Matt Seaton Meets JK Rowling," *Guardian Unlimited Network,* April 18, 2001. www.guardian.co.uk/ Archive/Article/0,4273,4171517,00.html.

57. Quoted in Seaton, "Matt Seaton Meets Rowling."

58. Quoted in Dunn, "From Dole to Hollywood."

59. Quoted in Malcolm Jones, "Why Harry's Hot," *Newsweek,* July 17, 2000, p. 56.

60. Quoted in Dunn, "From Dole to Hollywood."

61. Quoted in Fraser, *Conversations with J.K. Rowling,* p. 41.

62. Quoted in Smith, *J.K. Rowling,* p. 101.

63. Quoted in Smith, *J.K. Rowling,* p. 106.

64. Quoted in Smith, *J.K. Rowling,* p. 107.

65. Quoted in Smith, *J.K. Rowling,* p. 110.

66. Quoted in Smith, *J.K. Rowling,* p. 108.

67. Quoted in Smith, *J.K. Rowling,* p. 108.

68. Quoted in Smith, *J.K. Rowling,* p. 111.

69. Quoted in Smith, *J.K. Rowling,* p. 115.

70. Quoted in Smith, *J.K. Rowling,* p. 111.

71. Quoted in Smith, *J.K. Rowling,* p. 115.

72. Quoted in Smith, *J.K. Rowling,* p. 117.

73. Quoted in Hattenstone, "Harry, Jessie and Me."

Chapter 4: Poverty and Perseverance

74. Quoted in Smith, *J.K. Rowling,* p. 121.

75. Quoted in Smith, *J.K. Rowling,* p. 128.

76. Quoted in Hattenstone, "Harry, Jessie and Me."

77. Quoted in William Plummer and Joanna Blonska, "Spell Binder," *People Weekly,* July 12, 1999, p. 86.

78. Quoted in Hattenstone, "Harry, Jessie and Me."

79. Quoted in Dunn, "From Dole to Hollywood."

80. Quoted in Weir, "Of Magic and Single Motherhood."

81. Quoted in Plummer and Blonska, "Spell Binder," p. 86.

82. Quoted in Jones, "Magician for Millions," p. 59.

83. Quoted in Smith, *J.K. Rowling,* p. 123.

84. Quoted in Eddie Gibb, "Tales from a Single Mother," *Sunday Times,* June 29, 1997, p. 3.

85. Quoted in Fraser, *Conversations with J.K. Rowling,* p. 44.

86. Quoted in Gibb, "Tales from a Single Mother," p. 3.

87. Quoted in Smith, *J.K. Rowling,* p. 131.

88. Quoted in Smith, *J.K. Rowling,* p. 131.

89. Quoted in Anjana Ahuja, "Harry Potter's Novel Encounter," *London Times,* June 27, 2000, section 2, p. 8.

90. Quoted in Smith, *J.K. Rowling,* p. 131.

91. Quoted in Nigel Reynolds, "£100,000 Success Story for Penniless Mother," *London Telegraph,* July 7, 1997, p. 3.

92. Quoted in Ahuja, "Harry Potter's Novel Encounter," section 2, p. 8.

93. Quoted in Ahuja, "Harry Potter's Novel Encounter," section 2, p. 8.

94. Quoted in Ahuja, "Harry Potter's Novel Encounter," section 2, p. 8.

95. Quoted in Smith, *J.K. Rowling,* p. 136.

96. Quoted in Helen M. Jerome, "Welcome Back, Potter," *Book,* May/June 2000. www.bookmagazine.com/archive/issue10/potter.shtml.

97. Quoted in Plummer and Blonska, "Spell Binder," p. 85.

98. Quoted in Weir, "Of Magic and Single Motherhood."

Chapter 5: "The Pinnacle of Achievement"

99. Quoted in Weir, "Of Magic and Single Motherhood."
100. Quoted in Smith, *J.K. Rowling,* p. 143.
101. Quoted in Smith, *J.K. Rowling,* p. 144.
102. Quoted in Hattenstone, "Harry, Jessie and Me."
103. Quoted in Smith, *J.K. Rowling,* p. 148.
104. Quoted in Smith, *J.K. Rowling,* p. 160.
105. Quoted in Fraser, *Conversations with J.K. Rowling,* p. 46.
106. Quoted in Reynolds, "£100,000 Success Story for Penniless Mother," p. 3.
107. Nicolette Jones, "School's Out for Summer," *Sunday Times,* July 13, 1997, book section, p. 9.
108. Quoted in Weir, "Of Magic and Single Motherhood."
109. Arthur A. Levine, with Doreen Carvajal, "Why I Paid So Much," *New York Times,* October 13, 1999, section C, p. 16.
110. Levine, "Why I Paid So Much," section C, p. 16.
111. Levine, "Why I Paid So Much," section C, p. 16.
112. Levine, "Why I Paid So Much," section C, p. 16.
113. Quoted in Plummer and Blonska, "Spell Binder," p. 86.
114. Levine, "Why I Paid So Much," section C, p. 16.
115. Quoted in Weir, "Of Magic and Single Motherhood."
116. Quoted in Smith, *J.K. Rowling,* p. 153.
117. Gibb, "Tales from a Single Mother," p. 3.
118. Reynolds, "£100,000 Success Story for Penniless Mother," p. 3.
119. Quoted in Smith, *J.K. Rowling,* p. 155.
120. Quoted in Bertodano, "Harry Potter Charms a Nation."

Chapter 6: Pottermania

121. Quoted in Richards, "January Profile: J.K. Rowling."
122. Online interview with J.K. Rowling, *Scholastic.com,* October 16, 2000.
123. Quoted in Alan Cowell, "All Aboard the Harry Potter Promotional Express; an Author's Promotional Juggernaut Keeps Rolling On," *New York Times,* July 10, 2000, section E, p. 1.
124. Carla Power, "A Literary Sorceress," *Newsweek,* December 7, 1998, p. 77.
125. Gleick, "The Wizard of Hogwarts," p. 86.
126. Quoted in Gleick, "The Wizard of Hogwarts," p. 86.
127. Quoted in Elizabeth Gleick, "Abracadabra," *Time,* July 26, 1999, p. 72.

128. Quoted in Gleick, "Abracadabra," p. 72.
129. Quoted in Smith, *J.K. Rowling*, p. 162.
130. Quoted in Smith, *J.K. Rowling*, p. 163.
131. Quoted in Smith, *J.K. Rowling*, pp. 163–164.
132. Interview with Rowling, "This Morning Sunday Edition."
133. Online interview with Rowling, *Scholastic.com,* October 16, 2000.
134. Quoted in Jones, "Magician for Millions," p. 59.
135. Online interview with Rowling, *Scholastic.com,* February 3, 2000.
136. Quoted in Jeff Jenson, "'Fire' Storm," *Entertainment Weekly,* September 7, 2000. www.ew.com/ew/daily/0,2514,3590,00.html.
137. Quoted in Jenson, "'Fire' Storm."
138. Quoted in Jenson, "'Fire' Storm."
139. Quoted in Jones, "Why Harry's Hot," p. 54.
140. Quoted in Brian Bethune, "Harry Potter Inc.," *Maclean's,* July 17, 2000, p. 44.
141. Jones, "Why Harry's Hot," pp. 53–54.
142. Quoted in Bethune, "Harry Potter Inc.," p. 44.
143. Gray, "The Magic of Potter," p. 116.
144. Quoted in Auslan Cramb, "J K Rowling Denies Having Writer's Block over Next Harry Potter Book," *Telegraph,* August 10, 2001. www.portal.telegraph.co.uk/news/main.jhtml?xml=/news/2001/08/10/npot10.xml.

Chapter 7: Lights, Camera, Quidditch!

145. Quoted in Andrew Alderson, "They Really Do Look as I'd Imagined They Would Inside My Head," *Telegraph,* November 4, 2001. www.portal.telegraph.co.uk/news/main.jhtml?xml=/news/2001/11/04/npot04.xml&secureRefresh=true&_requestid=70396.
146. Quoted in Michael Sragow, "A Wizard of Hollywood," *Salon.com,* February 24, 2000. www.salon.com/ent/col/srag/2000/02/24/kloves/index.html.
147. Quoted in Smith, *J.K. Rowling*, p. 176.
148. Quoted in Sragow, "A Wizard of Hollywood."
149. Quoted in Sragow, "A Wizard of Hollywood."
150. Quoted in Sragow, "A Wizard of Hollywood."
151. Quoted in Jones, "The Return of Harry Potter!" p. 58.
152. Quoted in Smith, *J.K. Rowling*, p. 179.
153. Quoted in *BBC News,* "Young Daniel Gets Potter Part," August 21, 2000. http://news.bbc.co.uk/hi/english/entertainment/newsid_890000/890287.stm.
154. Quoted in Raffaella Barker, "Harry Potter's Mum," *Good*

Housekeeping, October 2000, p. 86.

155. Quoted in *BBC News,* "Potter Casts Spell at World Premiere," November 5, 2001. http://news.bbc.co.uk/hi/english/entertainment/ film/newsid_1634000/1634408.stm.

156. Quoted in "Potter Casts Spell at World Premiere."

157. Elvis Mitchell, "Wizard School Without the Magic," *New York Times,* November 16, 2001. www.nytimes.com/2001/11/16/movies/16 POTT.html?rd=hcmcp?=041VKn041VSs4MgnE012000mqEX DqEza#top.

158. Kenneth Turan, "Magic by the Book," *Los Angeles Times,* November 16, 2001. www.calendarlive.com/top/1,1419,L-LATimes-Movies-X!ArticleDetail-46658,00.html.

159. Quoted in Seth Schiesel, "Young Viewers Like Screen Translation of 'Potter' Book," *New York Times,* November 19, 2001. www.nytimes.com/2001/11/19/movies/19POTT.html.

160. Quoted in Tom Brook, "Potter Smashes Box Office Record," *BBC News,* November 19, 2001. http:// newsvote.bbc.co.uk/hi/ english/entertainment/film/newsid_1663000/1663560.stm.

161. Quoted in Brook, "Potter Smashes Box Office Record."

162. Quoted in *London Times,* "Prince Is Mad About Harry," March 3, 2001, p. 3.

163. Quoted in Smith, *J.K. Rowling,* p. 194.

164. Quoted in *BBC News,* "Potter Author's Content Warning," September 29, 2000. http://news.bbc.co.uk/hi/english/entertainment/newsid_944000/944728.stm.

165. Quoted in *People Weekly,* "J.K. Rowling," December 31, 1999, p. 87.

Important Dates in the Life of J.K. Rowling

1964
Anne Volant and Peter Rowling meet on a train bound for Arbroath, Scotland, from King's Cross station in London, England.

1965
Anne Volant and Peter Rowling marry; daughter Joanne is born at Cottage Hospital in Yate.

1967
Dianne Rowling, nicknamed Di, is born at the Rowling home at 109 Sundridge Park in Yate.

1971
Rowling writes down her first story; family moves to Winterbourne; Rowling meets Ian and Vicki Potter.

1974
Family moves into Church Cottage in Tutshill; Rowling enrolls at Tutshill Church of England Primary School.

1976
Rowling graduates from Tutshill Primary and enrolls at Wyedean Comprehensive School.

1979
Rowling learns about Jessica Mitford from her great-aunt Ivy.

1980
Anne Rowling is diagnosed with multiple sclerosis (MS).

1982
Rowling is voted "head girl" during her senior year at Wyedean Comprehensive.

1983
Rowling graduates from Wyedean with honors and enrolls at Exeter University.

1985
Rowling travels to Paris to study French and teach English.

1987
Rowling graduates from Exeter and gets a job as a research assistant at Amnesty International; she shares a flat in Clapham with other Exeter graduates.

1990
Stranded on a train in the English countryside, Rowling has a vision of Harry Potter; she starts outlining and sketching book series; Anne Rowling dies.

1991
Rowling leaves Manchester to teach English in Oporto, Portugal; begins writing *Harry Potter and the Philosopher's Stone*.

1992
Rowling marries Jorge Arantes.

1993
Rowling gives birth to daughter, Jessica; separates from Arantes; returns to Britain; joins sister in Edinburgh, Scotland.

1994
Rowling goes on welfare; lives in "grotty" flat; tells Di about Harry Potter; writes in cafés around town.

1995
Rowling completes *Harry Potter and the Philosopher's Stone;* types manuscript; looks up literary agents; Rowling enrolls in a teaching credential program.

1996
The Christopher Little Literary Agency accepts Rowling as a client; Bloomsbury Publishing accepts the manuscript for publication; Rowling gains her teaching credential.

1997
Rowling receives a grant from the Scottish Arts Council to complete *Harry Potter and the Chamber of Secrets; Harry Potter and the*

Philospher's Stone is published in Britain, and Scholastic pays $105,000 for its U.S. rights.

1998
Harry Potter and the Chamber of Secrets is published in Britain; *Harry Potter and the Sorcerer's Stone* is published in the United States.

1999
Harry Potter and the Prisoner of Azkaban is published in the United Kingdom and the United States; the book goes to number one in British best-seller lists; the first three books by Rowling hold the top three positions on the *New York Times* best-seller list; Warner Bros. wins the rights to make Harry Potter films.

2000
The *New York Times* creates a separate best-seller list for children's books; *Harry Potter and the Goblet of Fire* is published simultaneously in the United Kingdom and the United States in record first printings, becoming the fastest-selling book of all time.

2001
Rowling publishes *Quidditch Through the Ages* and *Fantastic Beasts and Where to Find Them* under pseudonyms Kennilworthy Whisp and Newt Scamander, respectively; the motion picture version of *Harry Potter and the Sorcerer's Stone* is released, setting one-day, two-day, three-day, and one-week box-office records and becoming the top-grossing movie of the year; Rowling marries Dr. Neil Murray in a private ceremony at a country retreat in Scotland.

2002
Harry Potter and the Order of the Phoenix is scheduled for release; the film version of *Harry Potter and the Chamber of Secrets* is scheduled for release.

For Further Reading

Books

David Colbert, *The Magical Worlds of Harry Potter*. Wrightsville Beach, NC: Lumina Press, 2001. An entertaining guide to the mythology and folklore Rowling uses in the Harry Potter series. This book contains fifty-three entries arranged in alphabetical order—from alchemy to wizards.

Lindsey Fraser, *Conversations with J.K. Rowling*. New York: Scholastic, 2000. J.K. Rowling's memories and musings presented in a question-and-answer format. The book contains reproductions of the author's whimsical line drawings, brief synopses of her books, and snippets of her interviews with *O: The Oprah Magazine, Newsweek,* and *Entertainment Weekly.*

Allan Zola Kronzek and Elizabeth Kronzek, *The Sorcerer's Companion: A Guide to the Magical World of Harry Potter*. New York: Broadway Books, 2001. An exploration of the history, folklore, and mythology that informs the world of Harry Potter.

Philip Nel, *J.K. Rowling's Harry Potter Novels: A Reader's Guide*. New York: Continuum, 2001. This informative guide to J.K. Rowling's first four Harry Potter novels features a brief biography of the author, a full-length analysis of the novels, and a discussion of their popularity.

J.K. Rowling, *Harry Potter and the Sorcerer's Stone*. New York: Scholastic, 1998. The first installment of Rowling's popular series, this book traces the life of a young orphan boy from his miserable life with his aunt, uncle, and cousin to his adventures at Hogwarts School of Witchcraft and Wizardry. There he makes new friends, learns magical powers, and encounters the evil wizard responsible for the death of his parents.

————, *Harry Potter and the Chamber of Secrets*. New York: Scholastic, 1999. In his second year at Hogwarts School of Witchcraft and Wizardry, Harry Potter finds himself in danger when an unknown power begins turning Hogwarts students to stone.

————, *Harry Potter and the Prisoner of Azkaban*. New York: Scholatic, 1999. During Harry Potter's third year at Hogwarts School of Witchcraft and Wizardry, Sirius Black, a wizard convicted of killing thirteen people, escapes from Azkaban, the wizard's prison, and threatens Harry.

————, *Harry Potter and the Goblet of Fire*. New York: Scholastic, 2000. Fourteen-year-old Harry Potter attends the Quidditch World Cup with his friends, the Weasleys, then enters his fourth year at Hogwarts School where he takes part in a special competition that tests his character, skills, and friendships.

————, *Harry Potter and the Order of the Phoenix*. New York: Scholastic, 2002. In his fifth year at Hogwarts School, Harry Potter enters a magical world unlike anything he has seen before and is forced to examine what death means.

Newt Scamander, *Fantastic Beasts and Where to Find Them*. New York: Scholastic, 2001. Written by J.K. Rowling in the guise of a famous wizard, this book describes imaginary creatures from the world of Harry Potter.

Kennilworthy Whisp, *Quidditch Through the Ages*. New York: Scholastic, 2001. Written by J.K. Rowling and designed as a volume from the fictional library of Hogwarts School, this book describes the history of Quidditch, the sport played on broomsticks by wizards.

Website

J.K. Rowling, **The Not Especially Fascinating Life So Far of JK Rowling**, (www.cliphoto.com/potter/rowling.htm). In this online autobiography, Rowling describes her childhood, her education, and her struggles at various clerical jobs leading up to the publication of her first book.

Works Consulted

Book

Sean Smith, *J.K. Rowling: A Biography.* London: Michael O'Mara Books, 2001. This unauthorized biography earned the wrath of J.K. Rowling but provides a thorough and well-researched account of her life. It includes reproductions of Rowling's birth and marriage certificates as well as good color photographs from her teenage and adult years.

Periodicals

Anjana Ahuja, "Harry Potter's Novel Encounter," *London Times,* June 27, 2000.

Raffaella Barker, "Harry Potter's Mum," *Good Housekeeping,* October 2000.

Brian Bethune, "Harry Potter Inc.," *Maclean's,* July 17, 2000.

———, "The Rowling Connection," *Maclean's,* November 6, 2000.

Judy Blume, "Is Harry Potter Evil?" *New York Times,* October 22, 1999.

Kerry Capell, Larry Light, and Ann Therese Palmer, "Just Wild About Harry Potter," *Business Week,* August 9, 1999.

Alan Cowell, "All Aboard the Harry Potter Promotional Express; an Author's Promotional Juggernaut Keeps Rolling On," *New York Times,* July 10, 2000.

Rose Cox, "Harry Potter Books Inspire New Love for Literature," *Anchorage Daily News,* January 26, 2002.

Maurine Dowd, "Veni, Vidi, Voldemort," *New York Times,* December 9, 2001.

Eddie Gibb, "Tales from a Single Mother," *Sunday Times,* June 29, 1997.

Nancy Gibbs, "Harry Is an Old Soul," *Time,* December 25, 2000– January 1, 2001.

Elizabeth Gleick, "The Wizard of Hogwarts," *Time,* April 12, 1999.

———, "Abracadabra," *Time*, July 26, 1999.

Paul Gray, "The Magic of Potter," *Time*, December 25, 2000–January 1, 2001.

Malcolm Jones, "Magician for Millions," *Newsweek*, August 23, 1999.

———, "The Return of Harry Potter!" *Newsweek*, July 10, 2000.

———, "Why Harry's Hot," *Newsweek*, July 17, 2000.

Nicolette Jones, "School's Out for Summer," *Sunday Times*, July 13, 1997.

Arthur A. Levine, with Doreen Carvajal, "Why I Paid So Much," *New York Times*, October 13, 1999.

London Times, "Prince Is Mad About Harry," March 3, 2001.

People Weekly, "J.K. Rowling," December 31, 1999.

William Plummer and Joanna Blonska, "Spell Binder," *People Weekly*, July 12, 1999.

Carla Power, "A Literary Sorceress," *Newsweek*, December 7, 1998.

Nigel Reynolds, "£100,000 Success Story for Penniless Mother," *London Telegraph*, July 7, 1997.

Internet Sources

Andrew Alderson, "They Really Do Look as I'd Imagined They Would Inside My Head," *Telegraph*, November 4, 2001. www.portal. telegraph.co.uk/news/main.jhtml?xml=/news/2001/11/04/npot 04.xml&secureRefresh=true&_requestid=70396.

Nigel Ballard, "J.K. Rowling Exclusive," BBCi, November 12, 2001. www.bbc.co.uk/bristol/content/feature/2001/11/12/jk.shtml.

BBC News, "Young Daniel Gets Potter Part," August 21, 2000. http://news. bbc.co.uk/hi/english/entertainment/newsid_890000/890287.stm.

———, "Potter Author's Content Warning," September 29, 2000. http://news.bbc.co.uk/hi/english/entertainment/newsid_944000/9 44728.stm.

———, "Potter Casts Spell at World Premiere," November 5, 2001. http://news.bbc.co.uk/hi/english/entertainment/film/newsid_1634 000/1634408.stm.

Helena de Bertodano, "Harry Potter Charms a Nation," *Daily Telegraph*, July 25, 1998. www.telegraph.co.uk/et?ac=001937575942258&pg=/ et/98/7/25/borow25.html.

Tom Brook, "Potter Smashes Box Office Record," *BBC News*, November 19, 2001. http://newsvote.bbc.co.uk/hi/english/entertainment/ film/newsid_1663000/1663560.stm.

Chat transcript with J.K. Rowling, *Barnesandnoble.com,* HP Galleries, March 19, 1999. http://history.250x.com/vaults/c105.htm.

Jeff Chu, "Christmas in July," *Time Europe,* July 13, 2000. www.time.com/time/europe/webonly/europe/2000/07/potter.html.

CNN.com, "Citing Witchcraft Theme, New Mexico Church Burns Harry Potter Books," December 31, 2001. www.cnn.com/2001/US/12/31/potter.book.burning.ap/index.html.

Auslan Cramb, "J K Rowling Denies Having Writer's Block over Next Harry Potter Book," *Telegraph,* August 10, 2001. www.portal.telegraph.co.uk/news/main.jhtml?xml=/news/2001/08/10/npot10.xml.

Elisabeth Dunn, "From Dole to Hollywood," *Daily Telegraph,* August 2, 1997. www.telegraph.co.uk/et?ac=001937575942258&pg=/et/97/8/2/bodole02.html.

Roxanne Feldman, "The Truth About Harry," *School Library Journal,* September 1, 1999. http://slj.reviewsnews.com/index.asp?layout=articleArchive&articleId=CA153024&display=searchResults&stt=001.

Simon Hattenstone, "Harry, Jessie and Me," *Guardian Unlimited,* July 8, 2000. http://books.guardian.co.uk/departments/childrenandteens/story/0,6000,340844,00.html.

Interview with J.K. Rowling, *Amazon.co.uk.* www.cliphoto.com/potter/interview.htm.

Interview with J.K. Rowling, *This Morning Sunday Edition,* Canadian Broadcasting Corporation, October 23, 2000. http://radio.cbc.ca/programs/thismorning/sites/books/rowling_001023.html.

Jeff Jenson, "'Fire' Storm," *Entertainment Weekly,* September 7, 2000. www.ew.com/ew/daily/0,2514,3590,00.html.

Helen M. Jerome, "Welcome Back, Potter," *Book,* May/June 2000. www.bookmagazine.com/archive/issue10/potter.shtml.

Helen M. Jerome and Jerome V. Kramer, "Author's Childhood Friend Says He Was Inspiration for Harry Potter," *Book,* March/April 2000. www.bookmagazine.com/archive/issue9/potter.shtml.

"J.K. Rowling Frequently Asked Questions." www.harrypotterfans.net/jkr/bio.html.

"Meet J.K. Rowling," www.scholastic.com/harrypotter/author/index.htm.

Melanie McDonagh, "A Magical Mystery Bore," *Sunday Herald.* www.sundayherald.com/19752.

Elvis Mitchell, "Wizard School Without the Magic," *New York Times,* November 16, 2001. www.nytimes.com/2001/11/16/movies/16POTT.

html?rd=hcmcp?p=041VKn041VSs4MgnE012000mqEXDqEza#top.

Online interview with J.K. Rowling, *Scholastic.com,* February 3, 2000. www.scholastic.com/harrypotter/author/transcript1.htm.

Online interview with J.K. Rowling, *Scholastic.com,* October 16, 2000. www.scholastic.com/harrypotter/author/transcript2.htm.

"Questions and Answers with J.K. Rowling," www.teachervision. com/lesson-plans/lesson-2693.html.

Linda Richards, "January Profile: J.K. Rowling," *January Magazine.* www.januarymagazine.com/profiles/jkrowling.html.

Shelagh Rogers, "Interview: J.K. Rowling," Canadian Broadcasting Corporation, October 23, 2000. http://radio.cbc.ca/programs/this morning/sites/books/rowling_001023.html.

Richard Saville, "Harry Potter and the Mystery of JK's Lost Initial," *Daily Telegraph,* July 19, 2000. www.portal.telegraph.co.uk/news/ main.jhtml?xml=%2Fnews%2F2000%2F07%2F19%2Fnpot19.xml.

Seth Schiesel, "Young Viewers Like Screen Translation of 'Potter' Book," *New York Times,* November 19, 2001. www.nytimes.com/2001/ 11/19/movies/19POTT.html.

Scottish Arts Council, "SAC Bursaries Enable Writers to Write," October 2, 2000. www.sac.org.uk/news/news_43.htm.

Matt Seaton, "Matt Seaton Meets JK Rowling," *Guardian Unlimited Network,* April 18, 2001. www.guardian.co.uk/Archive/Article/0, 4273,4171517,00.html.

Sandra Shulman, "Wizards and Ogres and Monsters, Oh My!" *Dish Magazine.* www. dishmag.com/current/celebrity/cc/10-p.3.html.

Michael Sragow, "A Wizard of Hollywood," *Salon.com,* February 24, 2000. www.salon.com/ent/col/srag/2000/02/24/kloves/index.html.

Kenneth Turan, "Magic by the Book," *Los Angeles Times,* November 16, 2001. www.calendarlive.com/top/1,1419,L-LATimes-Movies-X!Article Detail-46658,00.html.

Marina Warner, "Fantasy's Power and Peril," *New York Times Online,* December 16, 2001. www.nytimes.com/2001/12/16/weekinreview/ 16WARN.html.

Margaret Weir, "Of Magic and Single Motherhood," *Salon.com,* March 31, 1999. www.salon.com/mwt/feature/1999/03/cov_31featureb.html.

The Wizard World, "Scotland on Sunday: Rowling Mad About Biography." http://tww.darkmark.com/interview16.shtml.

Index

Picture Credits

About the Author

Bradley Steffens is the author of twenty-two nonfiction books for young adults, including *Understanding Of Mice and Men* and *The Importance of Emily Dickinson*. He lives in Escondido, California, with his wife, Angela, and his stepson, John.